Shifting

Out of
Chronic Stress

What others are saying about this book...

"Danielle has written a wonderful book. It's the rare combination of solid research, professional knowledge and personal experience that results in an inspired work of great wisdom. Danielle has committed to a process of deep personal exploration in her vision to help and support others who, like her, have suffered deeply from stress-related illness.

She has been fearless in her discovery and telling of the stories of her life experience and this has been crafted into wonderful pieces that enhance our journey as we read her book. I would warmly recommend anyone who has experienced stress or stress related illness themselves or through friends and family, to read this book. It is a relevant, moving and inspired gift that will help each and every one of us create a more healthy life."

—LISA BLOOM, INTERNATIONAL STORY COACH,
BEST-SELLING AUTHOR OF CINDERELLA AND THE COACH

"All of us experience stress in one form or another, and for some stress is a life long companion that erodes the quality of our relationships, the health of our body and soul of our spirit. It doesn't have to be this way and in truth we were never created to live this way. For the first time, an easy and simply applied 7 step process has been revealed by my friend Danielle Sax.

This book is for you or any person you care about who has had to live with the very real pain of chronic stress and it's effects on the mind, body and spirit. I have known Danielle for years and would trust her to work with anyone I care about. I know her heart, I know her desire to help, and I know her skill and ability as revealed in these pages."

—PAUL MARTINELLI, INTERNATIONAL SPEAKER AND TRAINER

"This book is written by someone who experienced stress first hand and learned how to cope. As a trained physiotherapist she applied her science and skills learned through her own stress experience to help others unable to cope. There are many useful tips in this well written and timely book."

–Professor Sir Cary Cooper, 50th Anniversary
Professor of Organizational Psychology and
Health, University of Manchester, England

"Danielle has 30 years of experience teaching, enlightening and caring for patients and clients living with stress. Her process has helped people to shift from chronic stress to a more balanced and happy life."

–Dr. Kathleen Hall, Founder, C.E.O.
The Mindful Living Network & The Stress Institute

"*Shifting Out of Chronic Stress* is a wonderful, creative book full of timeless insights and smart methods to help you de-stress, know yourself better and live a quality life. Danielle Sax writes from the heart as she points her readers in the right direction with elegant solutions, for a variety of life's challenges. I highly recommend this book."

–Bill Cole, MS, MA, Founder and President,
The International Mental Game Coaching Association

"As one who has learned to manage her personal pressure successfully, Danielle's book is a valuable, easy-to-follow guide of proven, stress-busting tips and ideas that can be used by anyone having to deal with excessive pressure over a period of time."

–Carole Spiers, CEO Carole Spiers Group.
VP International Stress Management Association UK.
Author of Show Stress Who's Boss!

For all those who have been my teachers through the years,
my family, my partner, my children and their partners
and every beautiful soul that crossed my path
for some reason.

And for all those who I am still to meet,
my future grandchildren and you, my readers.

Contents

Warning–Disclaimer

This book is designed to provide information on personal growth regarding shifting out of chronic stress. It is sold with the understanding that the publisher and author are not engaged in rendering medical, psychological or other professional services. If medical or other expert assistance is required, the services of a competent professional should be sought.

It is not the purpose of this manual to reprint all the information that is otherwise available to anyone under chronic stress, but instead to complement, amplify and supplement other texts. You are urged to read all the available material, learn as much as possible about shifting out of chronic stress and tailor the information to your individual needs. For more information, see the many resources in the back of the book.

Shifting out of chronic stress is not a quick-fix scheme. Anyone who decides to do the work must expect to invest time and effort into it.

The utmost has been done to make this manual as complete and as accurate as possible. However, there may be mistakes, both typographical and in content. Therefore, this text should be used only as a general guide.

Further, this manual contains information on personal development in handling chronic stress that is current only up to the printing date.

The purpose of this manual is to educate and entertain. The author and publisher have neither liability nor responsibility to any person or entity concerning any loss or damage caused, or alleged to have been caused, directly or indirectly, by the information contained in this book.

If you do not wish to be bound by the above, you may return this book to the publisher for a full refund.

Introduction

The World Health Organization calls stress the health epidemic of the 21st century. Employers all over the world rank stress as today's #1 workforce issue. Newspaper headlines talk about teenagers suffering from burnout and more people than ever before are feeling out of balance and seeking help.

My questions to you, dear reader:

Do you often feel stressed?

Do you think you might be "chronically" stressed?

I did not think so about myself. I thought that I was superwoman and that I was doing what I could and should to keep on going in these demanding times. As a woman, I took on the roles of a perfect wife, mother, daughter, sister, girlfriend and business woman, thinking that I was fine. I thought I was a bit stressed like everybody else. I assumed that being tired, losing my zest for life and often being anxious and overwhelmed was absolutely normal.

It is not. It is not at all normal. Life is supposed to be an adventure, fun, and challenging in a positive way. Your life should not put you in the position of thinking you "should" or "have to," of feeling pressure and urgency combined with the thought of "not being (good) enough" as you are. Do you feel any of these stresses? If you do, then you have picked up the right book.

My mission in writing this book is to warn people about the underlying danger of daily stress that can silently cripple your life. Stress is often a hot media topic, but "chronic stress" is ignored and neglected as the "real" cause of major physical diseases and mental problems that can affect hard-working, loving and caring people like you and me.

Is this kind of stress affecting you, too?

The physical symptoms of stress demonstrate that the connection between our minds and our bodies can no longer be ignored. Ongoing stress has a huge, undeniable effect on our bodies.

In the first chapters of this book, I will tell you my own story and describe my unique personal view on chronic stress. You will find that the judgement of others and the judge within ourselves feed our fears of not being (good) enough and that this is strongly encouraged by our education system. For those of us who are born as highly sensitive people, everyday life becomes even more challenging. That chronic alertness seriously endangered my life, and I have seen it affecting the lives of so many of my coaching clients in an extremely negative way.

Chronic stress is a silent killer. It affects your health, your daily life, your capacities in work and sports, your relationships, your family, your environment and so many areas that you are not even aware of.

Chronic stress depletes and destroys us. We cannot afford to leave it unattended or let it run its course. We need to treat it. We need to shift out of it. However, the quick-fix schemes do not work. There are no miracle cures; we need to start by addressing the cause seriously from within ourselves.

My intention is to show you throughout the course of this book how you can find the root of the stress problem, eliminate it or shift it and arm yourself with the strength you need to live without fear, judgement, shame and guilt. Through following my 7 steps, each explained in a separate chapter, you will learn to shift out of chronic stress and live the balanced life you desire and deserve. It is a method that works, again and again, because it addresses chronic stress at its core.

This book is about change. Life constantly changes, just like nature and the seasons do. But the changes I encourage in this book are changes, big and small, that come from within yourself.

These changes will follow a choice, a decision you make to finally do something about the stress in your life, for any of these possible reasons:

- [ ] *Because you have had enough of other people or external circumstances controlling you and your life.*
- [ ] *Because your body is telling you that you cannot handle your situation any longer in the way you have been until now.*
- [ ] *Because the balance between your work and your family has been completely lost.*
- [ ] *Because one of your children or grandchildren has made you realize that you want a better quality of life.*
- [ ] *Because you have heard one or more cancer survivors say that their perception of life has changed since receiving a second chance.*
- [ ] *Because . . .*

The fact that you picked up this book tells me that you are ready to take action. This book will guide you to make one little change that works for you, inspires you and motivates you to start doing things differently. You can start with one change at a time and begin to feel the difference.

Or, imagine that you take on the changes in all areas that are illustrated in each chapter, as a commitment to yourself. Day by day the small changes will become a huge change and, before you know it, you will have completely shifted out of chronic stress. I can tell you this for sure because I have lived it! This book will change your life.

"*Today is the first day of the rest of your life.*"

When you read this book and start to apply its content, you will automatically see the changes within you, in your inner world but also in your outer circumstances. The only thing you can change in your life is "you." Start to change your world by changing yourself. Make that commitment, read this book, apply its principles, do the exercises, talk about it in your environment and see what happens. It is by example that people around you will be inspired to act for themselves too.

"*You are your best investment.*"

Enjoy the ride and please feel free to contact me to let me know how you are doing. I sincerely care and look forward to "your" shift out of chronic stress!

Danielle

CHAPTER 1

The Moment of Truth

"If you do not make a decision, something or somebody else will make it for you."

My body did just that.

The morning of November 25, 1998, seemed like every other morning. At that time of the year, spring was in full swing in Durban North, South Africa. Waking up at 5:30 a.m., one could feel the oxygen in the air at the beautiful start of a sunny day. But these last months, after a very demanding winter, I did not take the time to see or feel that natural beauty, as I had too many worries about everything else that was going on in my life. I was living on autopilot, which seemed normal to me. I was responsible for so many things, and it felt as if I had to have it all under "control." I was living in my head most of the time, feeling anxious, restless and often in overdrive. I knew deep inside of me that I needed to slow down, but I did not.

My husband was already off to work and I started my race against the clock to get our children to school on time. Later that morning, I was planning to go to the Belgian Consulate to do some preparation for the coming

Trade Mission from Belgium (my part-time job). At 3 p.m., some PR work for my husband's company (my other part-time job) needed to be done. That night, I would make arrangements for the upcoming birthday of my youngest daughter and finish my day by keeping an appointment with a loyal client to give him a good relaxing massage, which was my specialty as a physiotherapist. It was a difficult financial period for our family, so I took on as much work as I could.

But first, on that particular day, I wanted to go to the gym to do my daily work-out, which felt like a "need" to exercise to stay in balance. Besides my family and my work, I was a very active woman, with a busy social life. I felt tired, exhausted even. Despite my intuition whispering to me to skip the gym today and go for a walk on the beach instead, I convinced myself I would probably feel better after a workout. I thought that I "should" work my body to be in shape, and it made me feel "good enough" to know that I had the right body looks.

I got to the gym around 8 a.m. and went for it. Toward the end of my 45-minute run, I felt a bit dizzy and by the time I was doing my series of strengthening exercises, my body got the shivers. Suddenly, I could not continue. I almost collapsed on the spot and felt extremely weak, as if I had a bad flu coming on. I sat down, tried some breathing exercises, but I could feel that something was really wrong. A friend agreed to take me home as I was not able to drive or walk properly at that point.

Within the next 24 hours, I was admitted to hospital with an exceptionally serious viral infection that showed up on the X-ray as a big black spot the size of an orange on my right lung. I was seriously struggling for breath, unable to sleep and could not "do" anything anymore, bound to lay flat on my back. But that was only the tip of the iceberg.

That first night in the hospital was my moment of truth, my red light. My body went into a complete state of alert; my heart was pounding out of my chest. I started sweating and became so anxious that I thought I was having a heart attack. I had a "panic attack" in the middle of the night, which lasted for hours since no medication could control my body or bring it back to its resting state. The fear of dying was real. What the hell was going on here? How had it come this far?

I went over the previous months and realized that there had been so many signs that I had not noticed. My intuition had told me so many times that I was doing too much. My mind had been racing and was not able to slow down. So many symptoms were running through my head. All signs were telling me to stop the rat race, but I never listened to the warnings of my body or my inner voice. It became clear that I had been living with chronic stress for months—even years—and now, it had completely shut down my body's immune system.

There and then I knew that turning this around would not take a day, not a week, not a month, but a very long time. I had been in complete overdrive for many months and was now seriously ill. Every fiber in my body was telling me that, although I thought I was handling everything well, this way of living lead to a dead end. I was slowly but surely killing myself. For years along the way, my body and mind had given me so many signals, and I had never listened, always feeling the "need" to go on. It felt as if I "should" care for and save everybody else around me while neglecting myself.

I realized that it was time to "stop," rewind the movie of my life and investigate my inner world. Time to consciously look into the real cause of my illness and to learn from my mistakes. I had no choice but to stop hiding

7

and pretending that all was well. Time to face the truth. Time to choose that day as the first day of the rest of my life. And so I did.

I have started this book with this story to warn you. Stress is a silent killer and at the root of so many diseases. Knowing what I know now, it was not at all surprising that my body gave in suddenly and dramatically from one moment to another. The mind and the body are so deeply connected. The chronic stress in my mind had a serious effect on my body. The body is so strong it can take and take and take until one drop makes the bucket run over. Then it may be too late or take a long time to undo the damage that has been done within the body. I sincerely hope this information reaches you in time.

More than warn you, I want to inspire you to "choose" to make a shift from within and end the vicious cycle of stress once and for all.

Questions for evaluating stress levels

So here are some questions for you to help you get a sense of what chronic stress feels like. If you recognize yourself in a few of them, see them as signals warning you that you are in the red zone.

- ☐ *Do you feel like you are living on autopilot?*
- ☐ *Are you finding it difficult to relax and enjoy yourself?*
- ☐ *Do you never stop thinking?*
- ☐ *Are you finding it difficult to say "no" to others?*
- ☐ *Do you take things that other people do or say personally?*
- ☐ *Are you living out of balance or only living for the outside world?*
- ☐ *Do you have low self-esteem or self-worth?*
- ☐ *Are you feeling over-stimulated or anxious in any way?*

☐ *Do you have a feeling of being too sensitive?*

☐ *Does your over-sensitivity leave you feeling depleted?*

☐ *Are you irritable, reactive or short-tempered?*

☐ *Do you have more negative thoughts and worries than you want?*

☐ *Are you feeling tired and exhausted?*

☐ *Do you always want to help, please and save others?*

☐ *Are you letting others make you feel guilty?*

☐ *Do you feel that your energy level has been too low for a while?*

☐ *Are you having trouble concentrating and staying focused?*

☐ *Do you have trouble falling asleep or waking up in the morning?*

☐ *Are you left with no time for yourself?*

☐ *Do you often start your sentence with "I should". . .?*

☐ *Are you feeling overall stressed and overwhelmed?*

☐ *Do you know what you desire and love?*

These questions may tell you if you are living with chronic stress, which can be destructive to you and your health. If you recognize yourself in these questions, you have picked up this book just in time. I know the feeling associated with each of these situations. I have been there. That's why this book can help you. More than that, it will heal your life from within–your internal world–so that none of the above situations will affect you in the future. The intention of this book is to shift you out of chronic stress. The 7 conscious steps explained in this book are tools that you can start to use and practice right away so that you will see an immediate effect in your daily life and a long-lasting result in every aspect of your life. But do not be fooled, this is not a quick fix guide. This 7-step process demands intro-spection, honesty, courage, self-discipline, perseverance and most of all awareness and practice. But it will be so worth it. I will guide you through every step of the way because it works miracles.

How do I know this process works miracles?

Because I have been there and have turned it around. Doctors told me that I would never be able to walk a flight of stairs again, that I would probably end up in a wheelchair and certainly would never be able to work again. Today I live in a beautiful home with stairs, I have a balanced life between my family, my friends and my work. My job has become my life's work as I do what I love and it fulfills my purpose.

Prioritizing my self-love and self-care serves me every day. I live out of unconditional love and joy with compassion and enthusiasm. For more than 10 years now I have been helping many people shift out of their chronic stress through my coaching, teaching, and speaking.

Because I come from a medical background, having studied and practiced physical and manual therapy for years, I know the body very well. However, it was through my illness that I discovered the essence of it all—the power of the mind, the mind-body connection and the importance of loving yourself and practicing conscious self-care.

By applying all these steps and bathing myself in a deep self-acceptance of who I am in this world while caring for my own basic needs, I have become stronger than ever before in my mind, body and spirit.

And so can you!

CHAPTER 2
A Different Way to Look at Chronic Stress

"The deepest fear we have, 'the fear beneath all fears', is the fear of not measuring up, the fear of judgement. It's this fear that creates the stress of everyday life."

—*Tullian Tchividjian*

As a physiotherapist, I was amazed at how emotional stress can cause serious physical symptoms such as headaches, back pain, and neuralgia, just to name a few. But only when I became sick did I come into contact with the reality of our mind-body connection. It is clear to me that the last 15 years of my life have completely transformed my view and understanding of stress. Having to deal with and heal from a serious stress-related illness myself, I was compelled to search deep within to find out what chronic stress was all about.

In this chapter, I will tell you about my personal view on chronic stress based on the first-hand experiences shared by myself and hundreds of those who have come to me for help. But before that, I want to briefly cover the basic classical understanding of stress.

The classical definition of stress

Being one of the richest societies mankind has ever known, is it not devastating to hear that we have never had such huge numbers of unhappy and "stressed" people on this planet? Stress is one of the words most frequently used in our conversations, research studies, articles, as well as being a popular subject of documentaries and talk shows.

When you look up what it means, you find numerous definitions and explanations of stress and stressors. It is not my intention to list them all, but I do not want to underestimate the complexity of stress in our world.

The classical definition of the noun is: "a state of mental or emotional strain or tension, resulting from adverse or demanding circumstances." Stress as a verb means "to subject to pressure or tension," and also "to focus attention on or to emphasize."

But how does the body react to stress? Where does stress originate from?

The origins of stress

Throughout the evolution of mankind, our bodies developed a mechanism with which to increase our chances of survival when faced with life-threatening situations. When a hunter came eye to eye with a big brown bear, he sensed that his life was in real danger. That trigger put into motion a built-in defense mechanism, which is a physiological process that enables the hunter to either "fight" or take "flight" or "freeze." It is commonly referred to as the "fight or flight response."

This fight or flight survival mechanism is a refined and effective system that involves our sympathetic nervous system, which is a part of the autonomic nervous system. In response to a trigger, the immediate response of the nervous system is to have specific organs like the adrenal glands and the brain produce adrenaline, cortisol, and norepinephrine. The release of these stress-related hormones and neurotransmitters results in an increase in our metabolic rate. Breathing and heart rate are accelerated, and we begin to sweat and become flushed. At the same time, the body's non-vital functions such as immunity and digestion are deactivated. During this process, more energy is created and more blood is distributed to the muscles, which is exactly what prepares the hunter to either fight or take flight. The body itself takes over complete control of all of its bodily functions. As you can see in the graphic below (Figure 1), once the sense of danger disappears, the body relaxes again and returns to its normal state. Although the triggers may be different in modern society, we react to our environmental or emotional set-offs in the same way as the hunter confronting the bear.

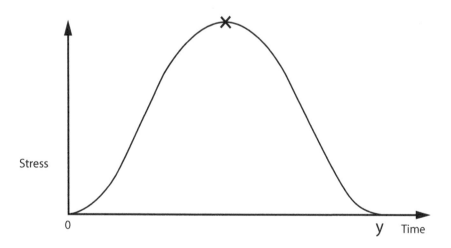

Figure 1

Our stress today

In today's world, we are rarely faced with life threatening situations. The fight or flight response is mostly activated by emotions.

The cause can sometimes be a positive one such as preparing for an exam, giving a presentation or competing in a final contest. Such a trigger is described as a "motivating positive stressor." It gives us the strength to perform, to get out of our comfort zones and just do it. Our hearts are pumping, we are feeling anxious and sweaty, and we are determined to make it work. After the performance, our bodies will come back to their natural state.

Unfortunately, for many of us, the inherent protective response is activated on a consistent basis by multiple negative and emotionally stressful events. We are exposed to consistent pressure to perform and to multitask in life. We constantly think of all the things we "should" be doing and the person we "should" be. Along with this pressure, there is a deep dissatisfaction and fear of "not being good enough." As we stretch to perform, we are continually demanding ourselves to function at our peak stress level. We find ourselves operating in day-to-day situations on a "chronic alert" level, never actually returning to our natural state of complete rest.

This lack of full relaxation has a detrimental effect on our bodies as there is no outlet for the biochemicals—adrenaline, cortisol and norepinephrine—and the extra energy that our bodies produce during the fight or flight response. This consistent injection of stress-related bio-chemicals weakens a person's body, which leads to a degenerative effect on our health.

Our brain, our muscles, our heart, our stomach, our bowels, our bladder, our skin, our sexual organs—every single cell in our body can suffer from continuous exposure to stress.

Chronic stress builds up over a longer period of time, often caused by multiple factors. It could be triggered by working too hard for too long, or perhaps having a job in an environment that is too demanding. Maybe you are living on autopilot and never setting reasonable boundaries. It could be that you always strive for perfection in your life and that of those around you, taking on other people's worries and accepting too much responsibility.

As you can see in Figure 2 below, when these situations persist, you never allow your body or mind to "come down" or return to your inert state of relaxation, or complete rest. You stay in continuous survival mode. I certainly did.

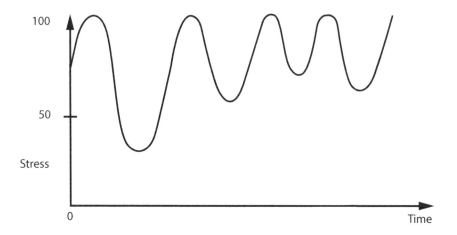

Figure 2: You can see a continuous peak of the stress level with only a few moments of 50% alertness and no moments of complete rest.

Exercise:
How about you?

Can you sum up your personal situations that have put you in continuous physical survival mode? Take a minute and write down exactly what it is in your life that is chronically too demanding? What depletes you emotionally? What makes your bucket run over so you become aggressive, oversensitive or indifferent? Or what makes you overreact regularly? You might encounter some or all of the situations explained in the list of questions in Chapter 1. Run through those questions again. Take your time and pick out those that are most applicable to you.

My personal view on chronic stress

In my experience, as well as in my practice, it is clear that "fear" seems to be the underlying emotion (energy in motion) of chronic stress.

Whatever stressful situation you are in at the moment—whether it be your job, business, family life, relationships, etc.—you can reduce it to an expression of "fear." According to Napoleon Hill in his bestseller "Think and Grow Rich," we humans have six basic fears: fear of poverty, fear of criticism, fear of ill health, fear of loss of love of someone, fear of old age and fear of death.

Although we might experience all of these fears during our lives, it is imperative to understand that in our society today, the fear of criticism (of "not being good enough") is the fear that is most dominant in our emotional lives. It is the fear that represents the underlying factor of most chronic stress.

Mr. Hill says: "The fear of criticism robs a man of his initiative, destroys his power of imagination, limits his individuality, takes away his self-reliance and does damage in a hundred other ways!" I can testify based on my life that this is true!

Of course, our fears of being ill, old, poor, lonely and also dying are very real. None of them can be underestimated since, they, too, can cause a lot of harm. I personally experienced the damage of the fear of poverty, ill health and death in a big way. But in our Western society, *the fear of not being good enough is the ongoing silent killer.* It truly is. I will explain to you why in the course of the following chapter.

As you read the following story in which I explain my life's lesson, see if you recognize anything in yourself related to your fear of "not being good enough."

My story—my life's lesson

I was born into a warm and caring home. Early on in my life a terrible tragedy happened to our loving family—the death of my little brother. I was five years old at the time. I usually played with him in the morning, before leaving for school. On this particular day, I got back home at lunchtime and found out that he had died in his sleep of "cot death (i.e., sudden infant death syndrome)." It was devastating seeing my parents, my older sister and the rest of the family so deeply hurt. One can call this a major stressful experience or trauma for a young child.

As an especially sensitive child, I felt responsible for the suffering within my environment. Unconsciously, I even took some guilt upon me and decided there and then that I would never cause any pain or suffering to anyone and would do everything in my power to please others and keep them safe. I would always try to be a "good" girl.

From that moment forward, in all the years ahead, I lived my life for those around me in my personal as well as in my professional life and was always putting myself aside. I did everything I could to receive confirmation that I was good enough because I did not feel that way within. I was aware of an emptiness in me that I needed to fill by taking care of others, with no boundaries, whatsoever! Most people around me thought I was fine, of course. I was bubbly, enthusiastic, optimistic and always nice and helpful; the one everyone could count on. I was hiding my pain, neglecting my needs and underestimating the stress it caused me. The fear of rejection, of criticism from someone else that I took so personally, was a consistent underlying mindset in everything I did. I was not good enough for myself, and so I believed I certainly was not good enough for others. I was convinced that I had to prove my own worth and that my self-care was secondary to caring for others.

It took many, many years for me to realize that I had integrated this unconscious belief of "I am responsible for the pain and happiness of others, regardless of my own needs" into my thinking as a 5-year-old sensitive child. Only then could I see that it was the basic onset of my long-term thinking and emotional patterns.

For years I was a people-pleaser, living for the outside world. I tried to be the person I was told I "should" be. My relationship with myself was everything but healthy. I did not accept or love myself. In fact, I was not feeling much at all, living mostly in my head while always trying to be good enough, smart enough, slim enough, etc. My relationship with food was unhealthy, and I was overeating, using food to fill up my emptiness. Sometimes I was also undereating so that I could control my body's looks or punish myself for not being good enough. At the time, I did not realize what all this was doing to my mind and body. I did not grasp that this underlying stress put me in a never-ending state of "alertness." Being alert enough to take the happiness of others onto my shoulders, and yet never being good enough, over and over again. Can you imagine how stressful ("stress-full") that must have been for a teenager and a young adult? Can you understand how the chronic stress-response was built up in my mind and body over the years?

Stress-full, yes, yet I was not "aware" of it consciously!

However, at the age of 38, the difficult financial situation my husband and I were in accentuated once more my fear of not being (good) enough, especially compared to others. The fear of not having enough (fear of poverty) was the last drop that brought about the onset of a stress-related disease (dis-ease). All the symptoms and signals had been there for many years, but I ignored them. I thought I was superwoman and could handle anything. Until that moment of truth! At that time, my whole being made me STOP and pay attention, whether I wanted to or not! I was forced to learn the lesson the hard way, lying down flat on my back. I could not sleep, eat or function anymore! For a long period, I was in a panic, a state of fear about what had happened to me.

Luckily I was a survivor, and I wanted to live instead of becoming a victim of my disease. I was determined to heal myself, regardless of what the doctors told me. My intuition told me I needed to go deep within myself, for the first time, and take charge of my life and myself. I needed to be honest with myself in order to change this self-created, sabotaging destructive pattern. Instead of obeying all of the "shoulds" in my life, I started to release myself from all conditionings, judgments, guilt and shame. I knew I had to learn to love and accept myself for who I was and to take care of my own needs first. So I started to practice Self-love and Self-care. These are not selfish acts; they are our birthright.

Yes, the tragic death of my little brother had had a huge impact on me, but the impact was magnified by my high sensitivity and the indoctrination of our education system. While reading the next chapter, see if you can begin to evaluate your own situation.

CHAPTER 3

The Effects of High Sensitivity and Education on Chronic Stress

"Educating the mind without educating the heart is no education at all."

—*Aristotle*

*I*n my experience, chronic stress often strikes highly sensitive people. In fact, many of my clients are highly sensitive and suffer from its effects, just as I have. However, it does not have to be that way. We can obtain great value from this beautiful characteristic when we know how to handle it correctly.

Chronic stress has also been severely enhanced by our education system. In this chapter, I will first give you a brief explanation of my view on high sensitivity and its relationship to chronic stress, and then I will explain to you in detail how the education system has contributed to chronic stress.

Are you very or highly sensitive?

It was only when my youngest daughter became seriously ill herself at the age of 13, that I realized she, too, had taken on that basic fear of "not being good enough." Psychologists told us that she was an extremely highly sensitive child. Only then did the puzzle fall into place for me. I realized that the path I had walked for so many years to heal myself was the same path highly sensitive people need to follow to free themselves from the burden of their sensitivity in this mainly prestige-driven society. Healing is the only way for highly sensitive individuals to finally stand in their light as they have a special mission in this world. Let me explain further.

Most people who are prone to chronic stress and stress-related illness are "very sensitive," if not "highly sensitive." They are born with an extremely well-developed central nervous system—even more so than usual.

Dr. Elaine Aron, author of *The Highly Sensitive Person* (HSP), is the doctor who originated the concept of Highly Sensitive Persons (HSPs). She described the complexity of this trait after completing and publishing numerous studies on the subject beginning in 1986. If you want to learn more about HSP, I recommend that you read her book, which I have listed in the Resources section at the back of this book. The documentary, *Sensitive, The Untold Story* will be soon available as a guide to understanding high sensitivity.

I would like to describe a few basic characteristics of high sensitivity in this book because it will explain a lot about the basic fear of not being good enough, which is something that very or highly sensitive people experience even more so than others. You may be able to feel for yourself whether this relates to you or not.

Firstly, take a look at the schematic (Figure 3) that gives a clear picture of how we function based on three main characteristics:

(1) First, Highly Sensitive Persons have a central nervous system that is extremely well developed, and they are susceptible to all triggers that come through their senses in a more intense and faster way than normal. For each person, the particular sense that serves as a trigger can be different. For example, someone may have a serious sensitivity to loud noises or bright or fluorescent lights or strong smells. Whether it be light or sound or taste or sensation or all of them that trigger you quickly and intensely, the overstimulation you experience can be either acute or chronic. This over-arousal will make you feel uncomfortable, anxious and even tired. Besides, you could feel overwhelmed by big crowds or noisy environments or over-stimulated when facing multi-tasking activities. Even violent movies might trigger you. Or you may suffer from certain allergies, which is the body's reaction to overstimulation of some kind. Multi-tasking, which is the norm in today's society, can certainly over-excite your system, resulting in all the consequences of a chronic stress response. You are unique in your own sensitivity, and so are your triggers that will set it off.

(2) Second, HSPs are born with an extremely well developed sixth sense by which they feel subtle energies and negativity around them. The illustration below [Figure 3] shows "feelers" or tentacles that

HSPs use to sense whether other people near them are doing OK. Thus, a highly sensitive individual will put conjunctions on other people and absorb all their negativity so that others will feel good. Highly sensitive people are like sponges, filling themselves with the suffering and negative energy of others, along with their unhappiness. At the same time, people within the environment of HSPs may feel drawn to them because they feel they are good listeners. Being highly sensitive, you may experience from a young age that people come to you with their problems, or you may sense when someone around you does not feel well. Some of us have the strong inner knowledge of what is going on in a particular situation. The pitfall is that we are so busy with absorbing all that energy that we get disconnected from ourselves.

(3) Third, and equally important is that HSPs have an inner urgency and desire to help, please and save people, no matter what. HSPs have such big hearts. In fact, an HSP "is" a big heart, which I have clearly illustrated in the drawing (Figure 3). Nevertheless, most HSPs forget to take care of their hearts. They will do anything to make someone else happy in order to feel accepted and worthy. As such, HSPs are the "good Samaritans" in today's world. They cannot stand injustice and do not like tension or severe rulings. They are born caretakers or/and exceptionally empathic leaders but often do not set their boundaries, depleting themselves along the way.

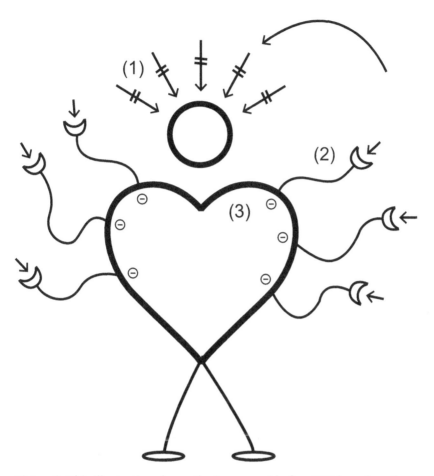

Figure 3: This illustration shows the inner world of an HSP based on the three main characteristics (1) (2) and (3).

Understanding the impact of our education and society

From the day we are born, we are a perfect bundle of love and joy, and we fulfill our basic needs by following our instincts. We have no filter, and so we take on and believe everything we are taught by our parents, our teachers, and society. We learn different symbols to be able to understand and communicate with ourselves and others.

Then our education system tells us that we are not (good) enough just as we are. Our parents show us what we can and cannot do and our teachers from preschool up to the last year of high school do the same. We are judged and punished for everything that we do "wrong" and equally judged and rewarded for everything that we do "right."

"Everybody is a genius. But if you judge a fish by its ability to climb a tree, it will live its whole live believing that it is stupid."

—*Albert Einstein*

This system of punishment and reward creates a basic fear of "I am not good enough as I am" so I will do everything to be good and rewarded and anything not to be wrong and punished. As a result, we get completely cut off from our core and from who we truly are. Instead, we live in our heads most of the time, worried and frightened, trying to be "good enough."

By the time we are half way through primary school, we have created a judge inside of us. We do not need others anymore to tell us what is wrong with us; we have imprinted the role of the judge and the victim upon ourselves. We constantly judge ourselves and others. We balance continuously in between right and wrong, playing a part instead of being who we are.

That in itself creates a consistent state of fear within us as we stop feeling who we are and what we want. The judge within us becomes stronger and can mutate into a monster, convincing us how bad and not good enough we are. Our mind does not stop criticizing and worrying, overruling all of our feelings.

The outside world (popular media, culture, fashion, etc.) confirms over and over again with a multitude of messages that we are not good enough. We are completely cut off from our core, our inner voice and inner child.

We only live from our heads, thinking who we "should" be and what we "should" do. We look outside ourselves for love and fulfillment and can never fill that emptiness within. (See Figure 4). Every day I see in my practice how we have cut ourselves off from our real feelings, from our "being." I see how we are surviving instead of thriving because we are living in our heads and not from our source, our true being. We are sacrificing our self-worth and self-care.

Figure 4: In this drawing you can see how the conditioning of our society and our education system has disconnected us from our core. We live in our heads, cut off from who we really are.

Looking at the illustration above (Figure 4), can you see the link between the fear of not being good enough that has been programmed into our minds from a very young age, and the chronic stress with which we live within this society?

I want you to realize that any one of us, sensitive or not, can suffer from all the consequences of this destructive pattern. This book is written for all of you who recognize that conditioning in yourselves. Chronic stress has become an epidemic and is a danger to our society. We develop many symptoms like headaches, constipation, insomnia, back pain, high blood pressure, just to mention a few. They can become illnesses like cancer, heart attacks, autoimmune diseases and so many others. More and more people of all ages are affected, and many also suffer psychologically. Some of them are only in their teens. Burn-out has become a daily topic in the news. It is time to treat the root of the problem.

The only solution to your inner struggle

The works of Louise Hay, Don Miguel Ruiz and other masters in personal development confirm that the fear of not being (good) enough is the only cause of major problems in our lives. To me, it is the only real cause of chronic stress in this part of the world. The only real shift out of this chronic destructive state is to go back to the basics. That is, to uncover all the layers of limiting indoctrination, to unlearn what you were taught about yourself and to re-boot the program you were born with so that you can return to your essence, your source, which is "unconditional love." In doing so, you will discover the freedom of being who you are meant to be. You will live out of love and practice loving self-care so that you radiate purity and lovingly help others from a place of empowerment, passion and purpose instead of sacrifice.

This is the only way you can make a real shift out of chronic stress and heal yourself completely. What I have just described is precisely how

I recovered from the effects of chronic stress myself, step by step, and it worked miracles.

What you will get from the chapters that follow

In the movie "My Greatest Teacher," hosted by the late Dr. Wayne W. Dyer, it is explained that nobody ever dies from a snake bite. A snake bite itself never killed anyone. It is just a bite. When you are in the jungle, you are bitten all the time. What kills you is not the bite, it's the venom. It is the poison that stays with you, circulating through your system long after the bite.

It is the venom that gradually destroys you unless you learn to get it out of your system, or you figure out a way to release it. Or even better, if you can find a way for your body to assimilate it. This would transform what was once toxic and turn it into medicine.

Here is the lesson: If you can look at the painful things in your life that have caused you the most suffering, you can figure out a way to turn them into your greatest teachers. This is what we are supposed to do for ourselves and the world around us.

In the following chapters of this book, you will find a step-by-step process to do just that. You can turn around the internal judgmental poison "of not being good enough" and turn it into your greatest teacher, shifting out of chronic stress and healing yourself completely. Each chapter can be taken on its own, but I do advise you to keep the sequence as it is structured because each step leads logically to the next ones.

My 7 conscious basic steps are designed to be balancing and healing. Each will have a serious impact on your well-being. They will transform your life from a stressful hell to a peaceful heaven as they make you take responsibility for your circumstances and go within to be honest with yourself. They will encourage you to focus on the essentials in daily life, using words of love and connection toward yourself and others. These steps are designed to reverse your destructive patterns/habits, replacing them with new empowering ones. Most of all, they will show you and teach you that Self-love is your birthright and that conscious, loving Self-care is essential for your health.

Step 1: Taking Responsibility for Yourself

Step 2: Examining Your Truth with Honesty

Step 3: Choosing Your Focus

Step 4: Being Aware of Your Words

Step 5: Developing Empowering Habits, Unlearning Disempowering Ones

Step 6: Making Self-Love Your Source

Step 7: Practicing Ongoing Conscious Self-Care

Each step has some interesting exercises that I advise you to take your time to consciously carry out. Simply reading a book will not "shift" you out of your chronic stress. Only practicing the steps and everything you read will make the difference you are looking for, and the exercises have that precise goal. It will all make a huge difference in every aspect of your life!

Remember to celebrate!

We do not celebrate ourselves and our accomplishments enough in our life. Instead of judging your actions and mistakes, start acknowledging and

celebrating who you are and what you do differently. . .anything that helps you to move forward and lifts you out of your struggle.

Lisa Nichols says: "What gets celebrated, gets repeated."

In this process of shifting out of your stress, it is imperative that you celebrate every single step forward that you feel you have accomplished. You can acknowledge a success after any chapter you have gone through, any exercise you have completed, any insight, any result, big or small. You can choose for yourself how you celebrate it. Even just playing your favorite song is a beautiful recognition you give to yourself. Or you can play the song and sing and dance full out. Or maybe you want to give yourself a little break and go into nature to enjoy some me-time. Every little choice or change that you have accomplished, celebrate it with yourself or anyone else for that matter. Celebrate your life at every occasion! Make a list of all the possible ways you can honor your shifts during our journey together!

I will celebrate with you, after every chapter, and every step along the way.

Are you ready and eager to start?

Step 1

CHAPTER 4

Taking Responsibility for Yourself

"The moment you take responsibility for everything in your life is the moment you can change anything in your life."

—Hal Elrod

Being responsible for oneself is one of the main characteristics of every truly effective, happy and successful individual. But do we understand its real meaning?

"Stop being a victim of your stress and illness, Danielle, you need to take responsibility for yourself." I heard this for the first time in a workshop on meditation during my illness. I was upset and furious. What did this mean exactly? My whole life I had been a "responsible" child, teenager, and young adult, as I described in my first chapter.

I found myself to be a very responsible person, always doing what needed to be done, always protecting and helping others as much as I could. I was a very responsible daughter, sister, girlfriend, physiotherapist, wife, and mother! I took the happiness and well-being of others onto my shoulders since I was a highly sensitive person. I even took the blame when things went wrong. I was also responsible for the unhappiness of others, always neglecting and forgetting my own happiness. I kept on judging myself over and over again for not being "good enough" when I did not succeed in making other people feel "ok" or when I made a mistake. If there was any responsible person on this planet, it was surely "me," I thought!

How could "they" say that I pretended to be the victim? Did "they" know what I had been through? Did "they" have any idea how bad our financial situation had been? Did "they" experience what I had experienced? How could "they" say that?

What did "they" mean by taking responsibility for myself? How could "they" even suggest that I, and I alone, was accountable for all my stress, my circumstances, and even my illness?

In that workshop, the teacher explained to me that we are used to living from the outside inward, meaning that we let everything that happens to us influence our lives and our feelings. The purpose of life is living from the inside out, which means choosing for yourself the life you want to create. Whatever the circumstances, you can choose from within your thoughts, feelings, words and actions. You decide, you choose. You always have a choice!

A whole new meaning

Unsurprisingly, the word "responsibility" took on a whole new meaning for me. I had missed the essence of this complex word my entire life. I always thought that responsibility was mostly about being responsible toward others. I never saw that taking responsibility meant becoming aware that we create our reality and our circumstances with our thoughts, words and actions. As opposed to letting our circumstances determine our state and our reaction to them. Taking responsibility is living from the inside out, meaning that you consciously choose what you want to create in your life. We are so used to looking outside of ourselves to identify the problem. Now, a whole new world opened up for me. My illness made me question everything I had believed in and taken for granted up to that point. It gave me the insight that Sophocles describes so well: "It *is a painful thing to look at your own trouble and know that you yourself and no one else has made it.*"

For a long time after this conscious shift within, I was depressed, sad and angry that I, me, myself, had created this. That I had let it come that far. Yes, it hurts to realize that I did that to myself.

Taking "responsibility" for oneself demands courage, a lot of courage. It is so much easier to stay in our comfort zone by blaming others or playing the victim. There is something in each of us that wants to avoid that responsibility. I did too. For so many years, I was living on autopilot, being and doing everything as I had been told and taught. I was not thinking or acting "consciously." All the positive things that happened in my life I saw as a blessing, as luck, as a reward for being a "good" person. All the negative things that came along in all those years were just "circumstances" and, with some of them, I was convinced they had happened because I had been a "bad" person, or because "they" did this to me. Isn't that what we are taught from a young age at home, in school, in our legal system and religious traditions? We are rewarded for being "good" and "nice" from the day we are born, and we are also punished for being "bad" and "naughty."

So, when the subject of "responsibility for my own self" came along, I realized that all those years, I had taken on a different responsibility: assessing myself by how "good" I was to others, taking care of them, pleasing them. I took that task very seriously. I enjoyed playing the judge, the victim and the blame game so much that it empowered me to ignore who I really was. It never entered my mind to look for the cause within me. I never grasped the fact that it all starts within ourselves.

When I did realize this, I went through a mourning process, as if I had lost a loved one. First I went into "denial," thinking: "No way did I do this to myself! Who would ever do this to themselves? It's impossible that I caused this to happen. This is not because of me. I always did my best in everything I did. I always took such good care of my body, eating well, working out and being a busy bee."

Then I went into "anger": "How can I be so stupid to have brought this on myself? How could I have been so neglectful of my health? Did I create this illness on purpose?" I was so angry at myself and at everybody else, realizing what had actually happened. For a while when I was ill, I gave a lot of power to my inner judge. What bad had I done to deserve such a punishment?

It was several months into that experience when I realized that all the self-judging and self-punishment were useless. I wasn't feeling any better. If anything, I was feeling worse. The self-blame didn't feel like healing; it felt like quicksand.

Do not blame yourself or anyone else

However, then I realized that taking responsibility for yourself has nothing to do with blaming yourself or self-punishment!

This knowledge didn't come overnight. It was a process and, to be honest, I sometimes still have to work through it. Initially, it's not easy for us to tell the difference between self-punishment and empowerment. We need to drop the habit of self-blame. We have just as much energy for self-compassion and exploration as we do for self-punishment. It's up to us to direct it and choose for which purpose we want to use that precious energy.

When I understood that, I started to feel the power of being self-accountable.

The day I could see and understand this truth was my first step toward healing and change!

Responsibility is about you, about being aware (without blame or judgment) that you shape your life and that you are the creator of your circumstances, of who you are, of what you have, of what you do and of what comes to you.

Do "you" blame your past, or anything or anyone in it, for your present? Or even for your future? Do you blame your boss for being unreasonable, your dad for being an alcoholic, the customers for expecting too much, or your kids for not listening to you, and on and on and on?

 Story:

A client of mine came to see me, explaining that she was suffering from a burn-out. She was running on empty. She was holding herself with rounded shoulders, face down, and I could see that she was exhausted as she dragged herself into my practice. Her story began at a young age, growing up with very strict parents whom she admired and adored. Her father wanted her to study law as he had done, and to become a lawyer. He told her it was a job with status and financial stability. However, she never really asked herself if that was what she wanted. She was intelligent, she could take up any study she wanted to, and so she became a lawyer, a very good one.

During our coaching sessions, it became very clear that she had hidden herself to make her parents happy. She became a lawyer in a big firm, yes, but hated it. All these years, she had done her thing as if she had no other choice. In fact, she said she would never have become ill if her dad had not "pushed" her into law school. She blamed her father, whom she loved dearly, for her present condition. She blamed her past choices, which she thought she had no control over, for her present. She blamed her partners in the firm for the pressure that she could not handle any more. She even blamed her past for her future as she was struggling to heal herself. She associated work with pressure and obligation. And she was not sure she would ever be able to work again. She saw herself as "the victim" of her circumstances.

When we talked about "taking responsibility for yourself," she reacted in shock. Because there she was, sick at home, blaming and judging everyone and everything for her condition. It was all about what "they" had done to her. She realized how she had held her father, her parents and everybody in the law firm but herself responsible for her situation, for her outcome, for her burnout.

It was time to look in the mirror and take responsibility for her choices, and for herself. She understood that she had to take her life into her hands and create her own conditions and circumstances. From that point forward, her life changed because she took back her power. She went through the whole coaching process, consciously, remembering and applying this very important first step. With each step forward she accepted her own responsibility in her creation. She has hardly ever spoken or acted like a victim again; she speaks her own truth. She has never felt so peaceful and relaxed. She is now studying photography and loving it. She has plans to open a gallery for artists and photographers, which was what she had always dreamed of as a youngster.

The first step toward change

Having the courage to take responsibility for yourself is the first "conscious choice" you make in this journey to a life of authenticity, freedom and inner peace. It is the first step in any change you want to make, and it is the essence of your foundation for happiness. We are created to be responsible. We are at our best when we handle our responses effectively; when we are "response-able" to whatever happens.

"Conscious" people know that responsibility is a choice that only they can make from within. They know that their response-ability is the capacity to choose a correct response in any situation they face. As a result, they tend to be very successful. However, just in case they aren't, they don't blame others. They are accountable for their actions and attitudes.

Now, does this mean that you have to turn your life upside down like my client did? Of course not, but it does mean that you need the courage to look in the mirror and reflect on what you see.

Your problem is not your job, or your spouse, or society at large, or anything else "out there." Turn it around. Your biggest challenge in life is YOU. If life's not going the way you want it to, you are responsible for making it better. And responsible winners do exactly that. They have the courage to "re-mind" themselves. The courage to investigate their circumstances and results as well as their focus, thoughts, words, feelings, attitudes, actions, habits, beliefs. . .all of which we will discuss in the following chapters of this book.

Accepting where you are now

I had a specific intention when I compared the decision process involved in taking responsibility for yourself, with the mourning process of losing someone dear to you. Because, now that you are past the denial, the anger and the blame, you get to the "acceptance" of things, just the way they are. It is imperative to realize that you cannot heal or change anything if you do not first accept how things are in this precise moment. Just agree that the place you are in right now is the exact place where life has led you until now. This place is perfect as it is however stressed and frustrated you may be, how wrong it may feel, how painful it may seem. . .this is where you are now.

From this moment onward, you are consciously going to choose your path; "you" are taking responsibility for your creation.

Happy people understand that their happiness is a state of mind "they" have chosen. They understand that no one can make them feel or do anything unless they allow them to.

Responsibility means freedom, and freedom means responsibility.

> *"Liberty means responsibility. That is why most men dread it so much."*
>
> —*George Bernard Shaw (1856–1950)*

Not taking responsibility may be less demanding, even less painful. It is certainly more comfortable in most cases. You can just take it easy and blame the problems and stress in your life on someone else. But do not be fooled! This attitude comes at a price, namely your personal power and freedom. You give away your health and your wealth.

I thought that taking responsibility for myself was going to give me even more stress. Nothing was further from the truth. The moment you understand this law of life, that you are the creator of your life, is the moment that you are capable of acceptance of where you are right now. Knowing that you can shape your own reality offers a certain inner peace. Because you now realize that you can change things, you can start reversing the process, handle your stress and heal. So, instead of being driven by circumstances and others while sitting in the passenger's seat or the back of your car, take your life into your own hands. Sit in the drivers' seat of your life, with "your" hands on the wheel.

Your life is up to you!

This is your life and no one else's. The rewards of being accountable for it from within are endless:

☐ *Your self-esteem receives an instant boost. And that on its own will create a different energy in and around you.*

☐ *Because you stop sabotaging yourself, you immediately start to be the person you want to be and to have the life you want to create.*

☐ *You take action from a place of consciousness. Instead of wishing and hoping for things to happen or change, instead of being passive and unmotivated, you are the active component that ignites the process you want.*

☐ *"If you take responsibility for yourself you will develop a hunger to accomplish your dreams." (Les Brown) You can start being the* person you were born to be as you will live from a place of awareness that gives you a better sense of your purpose.

☐ You understand that your responsibility has limits. You understand that you can't control everything in life. So you look at what is and see what might be next.

Lord,

Give me the courage to change the things that I can change

Give me the strength to accept the things that I cannot change

And give me the wisdom to know the difference between the two.

—Alcoholics Anonymous, Author Unknown

Responsibility means authority, power, influence and control. So reclaiming your power, the authority to be you, is mastering your own leadership.

Reclaim your inner strength. Decide to deal with your chronic stress, whatever it may be, by taking control of your mind and body. It all starts with taking responsibility for yourself; for your thoughts, words, feelings, actions, circumstances, and results.

Exercise 1:

Your turn:

Write down for yourself in which way you have not taken the proper responsibility in your life. Some questions that can help you:

- *What kind of responsibility have you taken on till now?*
- *Who were you blaming till now for your circumstances?*
- *What did "they" do to you? What was your part in this?*

- *Where in your life can you see that you need to take responsibility for yourself?*
- *Are you ready to take that responsibility from today onward?*

Exercise 2:
Visualization:

Close your eyes for a moment. Imagine yourself being an artist, a painter. See your life (from this moment on) as a white canvas. You have the paintbrush in your hand, so paint the life that you desire and strive for, no matter what the painting of others looks like. You now understand that you create your life every single second of the day, again and again, with each thought, word, and action. These are the colors that you can choose to paint with. My task for you is to decide here and now, for yourself, which colors (thoughts, beliefs, words, habits, etc.) you are going to decorate your canvas with.

Are they going to be neutral dark brown and blue and black? Or are you going to add fresh, bright ones like red and orange and yellow? Please grasp the importance of each color you are going to use as you create your own painting, your result, your life. You can also copy somebody else's painting or be influenced by someone else's colors. Is that what you want for your work of art, your life's work?

You are in charge; you are the creator, the artist of your painting (life). Are you ready to change the colors and make it an authentic reflection of who you are and the life you want to live? A happy, peaceful or passionate painting? Instead of a dreary and cheerless one?

When you have clearly seen the painting you want to create for yourself, open your eyes and take a deep breath.

Decide to take your paint box and canvas with you consciously, wherever you go. Take a "totem" that reminds you of this concept and commitment, so that you do not forget the importance of this first step.

Of course, you might encounter resistance since you have never played with this before, but just do the best you can in taking responsibility all day long without judging yourself if you make mistakes again. This is your life. It is nobody else's life and certainly nobody else's business what you choose to do with it.

Exercise 3:

Your summary:

Write down your summary of this chapter, of what you have learned about the meaning of taking responsibility for yourself. What have you understood from this chapter? By writing it down in your own words, you will integrate it better. I even advise you to explain it to the people you live with. The more you express your view on this or what you have learned from it, the more you master it.

Have you ever been told a joke that you liked but could not remember and retell? If you tell the joke at least three times afterward to someone else, you will have integrated it and will not soon forget it.

So, after each chapter, I will ask you to write down your summary and talk about it to others. It works!

♥ Remember to celebrate!

What exactly can you celebrate today? And how are you going to do that? Enjoy this moment of acknowledgement and praise yourself.

Please go to my website **www.shiftingoutofchronicstress.com** and let me know how you are doing. I will celebrate with you every step along the way.

Notes

Notes

CHAPTER 5

Examining Your Truth with Honesty

"Our lives improve only when we take chances and the first most difficult risk we can take is to be honest with ourselves"

—*Walter Anderson*

It might feel strange to you to read that being honest with yourself is the next step in this process. The reason I put such strong emphasis on this topic is because, in my journey, it was one of my turning points.

Honesty can be scary and confronting and can seem to give you even more stress at first. But it is clearly the logical thing to do after you have taken responsibility for yourself.

Now that you have done just that and have stopped blaming anyone or anything for your reality and stress, your mother-in-law, your boss, your partner, or your kids; it is time to look in the "honesty mirror." Have a look and ask yourself how your relationship with yourself is. Be open and transparent to your authentic self. It is time now to face the truth about yourself, your fears, your masks, and the limiting beliefs you hold that keep you from knowing what is really going on.

Ask yourself the following questions:

- ☐ Where in my life have I been untrue to myself?
- ☐ Which truth or truths are not my own?
- ☐ What role have I been playing, what mask have I put on?
- ☐ What is my real issue in life? What is the core issue here?
- ☐ What am I afraid of? What is my exact "fear"?
- ☐ What are my biggest doubts?
- ☐ Where am I not loving myself and accepting myself?

Honesty toward yourself correlates directly with how you deal with stress. You can ask these questions about even the small stressful situations in daily life.

Example:

You are stuck in traffic and you feel stressed. Why?

Are you sure it is because of the traffic jam? Or are there other reasons? Maybe something that happened the day before still triggers you and makes you nervous and impatient? Maybe your partner criticized you and you took it very personally? And so you still feel hurt or "not good enough," which makes you very agitated and short-tempered at this moment. Or are you feeling stressed and guilty because you have been told from a young age that "it is not good behavior to be late," and that thought of not being in control makes you feel anxious? Maybe your desire to be perfect and good enough is really strong, therefore, you do not want to be late?

Honesty is necessary to start the shift

I know being sincere takes reflection and courage, but please hear this:

One of my mentors, Paul Martinelli, an international speaker and trainer, talks about honesty and stress in his audio program "Power Principles." He says: "*If honesty is a systematic examination and embracing of the truth, that is what we need to do to become aware (of what stresses you and why). Only then can you start to change it!*"

He continues: "*If you are not living the life you like (and are living in stress), maybe you are living your daily life in less than honesty. . . .*" Once you look at it this way, you can embark on a completely new journey.

If you take living in honesty seriously and practice it consciously every day, you will feel more energized because being dishonest with yourself and others is draining your body, your mind and spirit. We may not realize it, but it takes so much effort to maintain masks and appearances.

Different aspects of dishonesty
– Who were you before the world told you who you should be? –

When I started to work on this first aspect of dishonesty, it amazed me to realize how we get so conditioned in our first seven to eight years of our lives by our parents, educators, family and culture, that we can very easily be dishonest with ourselves and others.

Just to please others and to get the attention we want or need so much, we unconsciously pretend to be someone else. We learn gradually from birth that it is crucial to be accepted and approved of by others. And therefore, we often slide into a role other than who we are.

In my own experience, I have realized that I took on the part of the perfect daughter, sister, friend, partner, daughter-in-law, therapist, etc., making decisions based on everyone else's opinions and expectations because I did not want to disappoint anyone. Instead of trusting my power and my inner voice, I became dependent on the judgment and approval of all those whom I wanted to help and please. I did not listen to my inner voice that was telling me what my own needs were, and I did not recognize my worth.

In our lives, we have created and maintained a cycle of stress and suffering, our own hell, by living in fear of what others might think of us, the fear of not being "good enough" always in the back of our minds.

Remember, earlier in the book, when we spoke about the "judge" and the "victim," that we decided to live for ourselves after we had been judged and victimized for years by others? It can be most interesting to look honestly within ourselves and ask who is in charge in different situations:

- ☐ *Is it the judge who is always watching and condemning you?*
- ☐ *Or is it the victim saying: "They are big and I am small and that is not fair"?*

Story:

    Marion, a woman who came to see me with many stress related symptoms, felt drained and exhausted as if carrying the whole world on her shoulders. She had weight problems. As a mom of two children with a full-time job, she did not have time to take care of herself. She worked six days out of seven as a partner in a carpet company that she ran together with her husband. In our conversation, she often began statements with "I should. . ." which made it evident to me that she was constantly judging herself and punishing herself for all that she "should" be, do and have. She was convinced that her stress was caused by not having enough time in the day to do what she was supposed to do. She asked me to help her with time-management skills and tips to get her situation solved so that she could regain her work-life balance. In her opinion, those tips would resolve her stress since she would then be able to do what she should or had to do.

When I gave Marion the mirror of honesty so that she could uncover the real truth of her stress, she realized that she was living completely out of balance with herself. She had buried that little Marion a long time ago when her mother had more of an eye for her brother than for her. And she felt that she never received any approval or appreciation. Therefore, she did everything to be the perfect daughter, sister, etc. She lived for the outside world, forgetting her own basic needs and always trying to please everyone in her environment and doing what she "had" to do, what she "should" do instead of what she wanted to do. Not feeling complete, and not feeling worthy, she filled herself up with comforting food, creating a weight problem. Although she thought her stress came from her poor time management, she was stressed because she did not feel good enough, and not worthy of love for who she was. That was her real stressor!

Being honest with yourself takes inner guidance and introspection, but it is so worth it. Once you know what is really going on, you can start to heal the real stressor!

– What beliefs do you have about yourself and your world? –

"Stress and emotional pain is not caused by the external issues but by the battle between who you really are and the false ideas you've been brainwashed to believe about yourself."

—Derek Rydall

A second aspect of dishonesty involves the "beliefs" we adopted from the people around us when we were growing up. Beliefs are the opinions of others that we have internalized as the truth, either about ourselves, the world, society or anything else under the sun. We are what we believe to be. Most of those beliefs are seriously limiting since they prevent us from standing in our authenticity and light. So, what do "you" believe yourself to be? We assume that what others tell us and what we believe represent the truth. But is this really the truth? What "is" the truth?

Are you dependent on the recognition and approval of others? Are you sensitive to their opinions and confirmation? Then, what you are about to read now might shock you: What others say and do is "their truth," and has nothing to do with "you" in the first place. We will discuss this in more detail in the chapter on habits, in which I explain why it is not advisable to take anything for granted or to take anything personally.

So, if we always see "the truth" in what others tell us, we start believing and embodying it. We take over those convictions and they rule our world.

Behind your conscious beliefs, you have installed some unconscious beliefs in those first years of your life during your conditioning and indoctrination. What exactly did you (or do you) believe about yourself, or about love, money or anything that matters to you? Your environment made you download certain convictions about yourself that you took in as the truth, again and again.

The most frequent subconscious limiting beliefs are these three:

- ☐ *If I try, I will fail.*
- ☐ *No one wants me.*
- ☐ *I'm not worthy.*

These all come down to the basic acknowledgement and fear of not being good enough. Perhaps you can begin to see how important it is to identify your own restrictive convictions and then question the truth about them?

"Man is what he believes"

—*Anton Chekhov*

Our lives proceed from our beliefs. This means that your life, and how you perceive everything, is dominated mostly by the beliefs that you learned about yourself and the world. And those beliefs conceive your story, your emotions and your experience as you live your reality. We create our experience, and the architect is our belief system. We become what we "think" we are, through the eyes of others.

Story:

A client of mine felt a considerable amount of stress when he had to speak in front of others or give his opinion to others. He was a senior manager and was highly intelligent and compassionate. He had many good qualities but experienced many symptoms of stress while dealing with people and various interactive situations. In business meetings, he found it difficult to stand up for his own findings, always waiting until everybody else had given their comments and then talking from a place of inferiority.

While doing the honesty work with this client, aged 48, he discovered that his mother had told him at a young age to "shut up" because he was not able to speak as fluently as his brother and sister. He believed this and got anxious because he thought other people would judge him or think poorly of him (as he felt his mother did). He did not feel good enough about himself because of what his parents had told him so many years before. "You are not good enough at speaking." That opinion had become an integrated belief and was responsible for creating major trauma in his life.

Now, that may sound ridiculous at first but think about it. How many things have you believed that were true about you that were the opinions of someone else? As motivational speaker Les Brown has stated: "*Someone's opinion of you does not have to become your reality.*"

Our beliefs about who and what we are, need to be investigated "honestly" so they can be replaced by our truth and authentic potential. Because there is only "one opinion" about you that is of value to you and that is the opinion you have about yourself.

We often think that being truthful is about "not lying to others," but in this journey of conscious decisions, it is so much more. Honesty has everything to do with the way you relate to yourself, your intentions and your integrity, in addition to how you relate to other people.

– Our addictions –

"All the suffering, stress and addiction comes from not realizing you already are what you are looking for!"

—*Prem Prakash*

A third example of dishonesty with yourself manifests itself as an addiction. The biggest addiction in society today is that of suffering. Yes, many of us are addicted to drama and problems. However, suffering is created in the human mind and it is an option, a choice. Many people need to suffer to feel alive. This irrational, emotional agony is neither necessary nor normal. Suffering to some extent seems normal since we grew up with it and we see everybody around us subjected to it. Take a look at your basic fear of not being good enough and then consider the lingering pain it has created in your life. Can you understand how important it is to stop having this irrational conditioned fear?

Most of the other addictions we have come from this basic mindset of fear, whether it is about food, alcohol or drugs, whatever the addictive behavior might be. You could even be addicted to watching TV or using your iPad or working out at the gym. In this society, in which we are more bored than ever, we stay busy distracting ourselves from the truth of our lives through social networking and electronic communication, which are ways of displaying who we are for the outside world to see.

When it comes to addiction, the steps toward healing can only be taken by being truly honest with yourself, when nobody is watching, and admitting that there is a problem. You can then dig deeper within and find out what the real problem is at the root of your addiction. This is where the power of honesty resides!

Being your authentic self

Honesty and authenticity are integrally connected to each other. To me, not being authentic means that you are not being true to who you are and not expressing your unique self. There is nothing worse than self-betrayal. In this journey of deliberate choices, it takes courage and consciousness to be authentic.

Staying true to yourself, listening to your inner voice, to your mind and body is imperative in order to find inner peace again.

Unfortunately, I only started doing that when I "had" to. One of the main reasons my body gave in on that November morning in 1998 was because I had been dishonest with myself for many years. Not only had I sacrificed myself for the approval and well-being of others, I also ignored the signals of my dishonesty again and again.

I had been living for months (even years) in discontent and disconnection with myself. My intuition had told me so many times that I was off track.

My mind was screaming every day with unhealthy negative thoughts, but I assumed that this was normal. My body had given me so many signals, including fatigue, muscle pain, inflammation, and more, but I did not listen. And I paid a big price for it!

"Everyone knows the truth, no matter how long they have been lying about it."

—Author unknown

In my practice, I see people every day who need to go through a "crisis" before they start being honest with themselves. Is that you?

Of course, it is not possible to be true to yourself unless you know your own "truth." To know your truth, you have to be willing to discover it yourself. Even more so, you have to be ready to uncover the naked relationship you have with yourself. You have to reflect on and evaluate your beliefs and see how they have shaped your life. Start today to be honest with yourself and examine your truth, and I promise you will experience a major shift.

Being your authentic self can seem like a tough road to walk at first. This is quite amazing, because being ourselves should be the "easiest" road to walk. You might encounter some resistance along the way as you get out of your comfort zone. But you will begin to feel so free when you no longer have to do so much to please others. Your life is now completely up to "you"! You can create anything you want. Begin to uncover and discover the honest truth about yourself. It is the only way to the road of consciousness and authentic creative power.

Do not wait until your symptoms of stress become worse or your body and mind shut you down. Start being honest with yourself today, now, without hesitation.

Step into your own truth, into your own light. So often we are blind to it! From the day we are born, we have been shown what our inadequacies are and how imperfect we are. It is time to stand in your true value and bring your light to the world, regardless of any shortcomings you might have.

"Our deepest fear is not that we are inadequate. Our deepest fear is that we are powerful beyond measure. It is our light, not our darkness that most frightens us. We ask ourselves: Who am I to be brilliant, gorgeous, talented and fabulous? Actually, who are you not to be?

You are a child of God. Your playing small does not serve the world. There is nothing enlightened about shrinking so that other people won't feel insecure around you. We are all meant to shine, as children do. We were born to make manifest the glory of God that is within us. It's not just in some of us; it's in everyone.

And as we let our own light shine, we unconsciously give other people permission to do the same. As we are liberated from our own fear, our presence automatically liberates others."

—Marianne Williamson

Exercise 1:

Examine your beliefs about yourself

Write down for yourself five words that describe you: "I am _____."
These are five mental labels that you gave to yourself or that someone
else gave to you. You took ownership of these labels and this is your truth
now. Go within and be honest with yourself. Ask questions and stay close
to who you are. Be quiet and listen. When you are honest enough to ask
yourself quality questions, you will get quality answers and spare yourself
much suffering.

Some questions that may help you:

- Which belief of mine is making me suffer?

  Example: "I am just average." It gives me low self-esteem.

- Where does the idea come from? Whose opinion is it?

  Example: "My teachers at school always told me that I was average."

- Can I let go of this belief and step into my own truth?

  Example: "Is this really true, am I always average? Is this who I am?"

- What do I honestly think of myself?

  Example: "I am maybe average in things like cooking and science,
  but at the same time, I am talented and brilliant in other things like
  languages and social skills."

- What will my life look like starting today if I intend to live in honesty
  with myself and others?

  Example: "I will feel much more confident in who I am, and in how
  I appear to others."

Exercise 2:
Grounding Yourself

When you are grounded and feeling supported by the earth under your feet, it is much easier to be honest from within and to be true to yourself.

Sit in a quiet place where you cannot be disturbed. Maybe in the corner of your favorite room with a view, maybe outside in nature where you feel close to yourself, or anywhere you choose as long as you feel comfortable.

Close your eyes and keep your hands loosely on your lap, with your feet touching the ground. Breathing deeply, drawing air into your tummy for a minute and letting it out again, and feel a peace coming over you.

Bring your attention to your feet and visualize yourself being a tree with the roots growing from your feet deep into the earth underneath you. Imagine the roots go as deep and as large as you can. Sense how they empower you. Feel your strength. Be grateful for your grounding as it is there only for you. When you are ready, you can open your eyes and come back into the here and now feeling fully grounded.

Exercise 3:
Your summary:

Write down your summary of this chapter, of what it means to be honest with yourself from within. What have you picked up from this chapter that is new to you? What have you learned about yourself?

By writing these things down in your own words, you will integrate what you have learned effectively. I even advise you to explain it to the people you live with or your friends. The more you express your own view on this or what you have learned from it, the more you will master it.

Remember to celebrate!

What exactly can you celebrate today? And how are you going to do that? Enjoy this moment of acknowledgement and praise yourself.

Please go to my website **www.shiftingoutofchronicstress.com** and let me know how you are doing. I will celebrate with you every step along the way.

Notes

Notes

Step 3

| | CHAPTER 6

Choosing Your Focus

"Make sure that what you are focusing on serves you."

—*Cherie Roe Dirksen*

*E*very change starts with a choice, a decision. The choice of focus might be one of the most important decisions you ever make in handling your stress and finding peace within yourself.

Focus is your centre of interest, your focal point. To focus on something means to sharpen your attention, to concentrate your attention and to not let yourself be distracted.

Our brain is like a camera and our experience is based on the focus of that camera. What is "your" brain paying attention to? We need to train our brains to be alert to what we "want" to experience. From my life experience and from what I hear from others, it is clear that focus needs to be directed consciously. To what do you choose to give your particular attention?

It is all too easy, when dealing with a stressful situation, to perceive it as negative and threatening and to focus on all the negativity that comes with it. That, on its own, can be damaging. Some of us may also encounter a certain lack of focus, which creates a negative reality and scarcity since there is no plan or purpose. Both are stressful; we either have a lack of focus or we are focusing on the wrong things.

A lack of focus

Let me give you an example of how easy it is to lose focus. When I decided to write this book, which is a long overdue dream, it took me a few months before I realized that I was not getting anywhere. I was often stressed out because I truly wanted to write this book, but I always found a reason to procrastinate. Whether it was a telephone call, mails to answer, household tasks to be done or even a friend inviting me for lunch—some distraction always made me postpone the actual writing. I was irritable, tired from doing everything and nothing, always busy but never getting anything done. As Les Brown says: "*We are victims of mass-distractions, not mass-destructions. It is hard to keep your mind focused and single.*"

Focus is the point at which rays of light, heat and sound converge. So when I decided to take on a coach to guide me, to set up my plan and keep my focus, that was when my writing started flowing. I blocked time to write into my schedule and put all other tasks and distractions aside. I directed my focus based only on my priority, on my goal for this year, which gave me the discipline to take action several hours a day. In line with my experience, I advise you to focus on what you truly want in life, not on all the things in between.

Focusing on the wrong things:

"People are disturbed, not by a thing, but by their perception of a thing."

—*Epictetus*

The way you look at things determines how you experience them. Your perception is your filter, and that may or may not cause you stress. Your perception is more important than the event itself. How you "view" that potentially stressful event will be the largest single factor that has an impact on your mental and physical health. So, your interpretation of situations and challenges in life may decide whether they are harmful to you or not.

"We can complain because rose bushes have thorns or rejoice because thorn bushes have roses."

—*Abraham Lincoln*

The way you perceive your reality as being either good or bad, positive or negative, determines whether you feel happy or sad. This chapter on focus presents a vital step in shifting out of chronic stress. Oprah Winfrey says: *"The smallest change in perspective can change a life. What tiny attitude adjustment might turn your world around?"*

It is worth investigating where your own focus lies in your daily life. What receives your attention most of the time?

– Do you focus on the absence or lack of something? –

Which glasses are you looking through? Are you focused, as many people are, on what you cannot be, cannot have, cannot do? Are you paying special attention to the absence or lack of all things, instead of to the presence or abundance of those things?

I see it in my practice every day. People compare themselves with others or focus on their shortcomings or failures, rather than concentrating on their talents or successes. From childhood, some of us have focused on the mistakes we have made instead of being motivated and congratulated for our talents and uniqueness. Remember when you came home with a report card that had grades A and A+, and one B– on it? Where did your parents' attention go?

The ultimate failure in life is to linger over something that does not match our expectations. We can always choose to focus on the pain in something, no matter how good it is. Success is our ability to find the good in life, no matter how painful it is, creating consistent growth and pleasure. You can focus your mind on anything you choose, so highlight the positive things in your reality and that mind-set will certainly make a difference in your life.

– Do you focus on the past and the future? –

"Only we humans worry about the future, regret the past and blame ourselves for the present."

—Rick Hanson

Most of us are always thinking of what has happened or what might happen. That is why we lose our energy; we are not living in the present. If you are dwelling on the past, you are not staying close to yourself, you are not grounded in the here and the now. Sometimes you may be spending all of your energy on things that you cannot change anymore. Yes, you made mistakes, but the past lies behind you.

As we covered in Chapter 4, "Taking responsibility for yourself," it is important to distinguish what we can and cannot change in the here and the now. Whatever you did in the past is gone. The only question to ask yourself is: Do I need to accept this or can I change this by taking a different action today to create another outcome in the future?

Happy people focus on their potential rather than their current results. They understand that their results are only a reflection of their past, which was based on their awareness of their potential at that time.

If you are constantly worrying about the future, about "what might happen if," then you are using your imagination to create worry. Focusing your attention on things you cannot control will give you anxiety and stress. You will then miss out on the essence of life, which is this moment, now. We call it the present because it is a gift.

If there is one thing certain in life, it is that life is uncertain. So life is an adventure, if you choose to see it that way.

– A special note and a story about "worry" –

The question "What if?" can create drama and hell in your life.

When you look at the essence of your worries, how solid are they? It transpires that 95% of our anxiety and worry is about things that never happen to us or others, and only 5% of our daily fears can truly be justified. Therefore, 95% of the time we are wasting our energy by worrying for nothing. In fact, it is depleting us so much more than we realize. Go back to having "faith." See the possibilities and miracles. Stop worrying!

Consider these acronyms:

FEAR= False Evidence Appearing Real

FAITH= Full Awareness In The Heart

Illustrating story:

A little girl walked to and from school every day. Though the weather on one particular morning was unstable and clouds were forming, she still made her daily trip to school. As the afternoon progressed, the winds whipped up, along with thunder and lightning.

Her mother felt concerned that her little one would be frightened as she walked home from school, and she feared that the electrical storm might harm her child. Following the roar of thunder and the flash of lightning through the sky, the mother, full of anxiety, quickly got into her car and drove along the route to her daughter's school.

As she did so, she saw her little girl walking along, and at each flash of lightning, the child would stop, look up and smile. One quickly followed after the other, and every time the little girl stopped, looked up and smiled.

Finally, the mother called over to her little girl and asked: "What are you doing?" The child answered smiling: "God just keeps taking pictures of me!"

This story is about worry, but it tells us more about "faith."

– Are you making assumptions? –

How often do we "think too much," meaning that we make assumptions? Thinking too much creates fear. A great deal of doubt and fear is also produced by the assumptions we make in our heads of "what could be." By assuming what happened or what "might" happen, we misinterpret and misunderstand everything. We start imagining what other people are thinking or saying about us. And that imagined scenario takes on a life of its own. We invent a whole story around it, and that story becomes true for us. We believe a story that was only based on an assumption.

Don Miguel Ruiz, the Toltec spiritualist and author, explains in "The Four Agreements" that because it is so easy for us to make assumptions about the meaning of something, we create considerable suffering for ourselves. Stressful situations are so often based on a sequence of assumptions since one usually leads to another. On top of that, we often take things personally and so our energy becomes judgemental, resentful and blameful. We are often too afraid to ask for clarification. Therefore, we assume we know the truth, not realizing that it is, in fact, a lie. Because we "believe" we are right, we then defend our assumption.

We will even destroy relationships based on assumptions we hold in our minds. Instead of causing a wave of poisonous thoughts, we can ask ourselves or others questions before coming to conclusions. So, have the courage to ask questions until it is clear to you what the real truth is, and not what we "think" it to be.

Example:

For the 3rd time this week, your partner comes home and sits in the living room instead of coming to speak to you. When this happens, you might assume: Here we go again, he/she comes home and is not even interested in how my day went. You start making assumptions that bring you to the conclusion that maybe he/she is upset with you or does not love you anymore. (No, this is not exaggerated. I often hear in my practice how people make up huge dramas in their heads, all based on an assumption). The drama is surely going on in your head. Instead, if you asked him/her directly with a caring voice why he/she first needs to sit in the living room when he/she comes home, he/she might give you the real reason. Maybe it's because he/she has had a conflict with his/her boss at work or perhaps it's because he/she has not slept well this week and has a headache. The truth is, until you ask him/her, you do not know. It is good to ask questions, instead of making up assumptions in your head. We think we know, but we don't.

– Do you focus on the problem instead of the opportunity? –

Problems are not stop signs; they are guidelines.

Maybe you are seeing everything that happens to you as a "problem," and consider it to be impossible to overcome. Les Brown has stated that the word *Impossible* means *I'm possible*. Everything is possible. Sometimes, taking a helicopter view of a situation can shift your whole perception. In contrast, when you stay in the middle of the storm, you cannot be objective and see what is truly happening. Take yourself out of the situation and look at it from a distance. Only then can you see the opportunity in disguise.

> *"Every adversity, every failure, every heartache carries with it the seed of an equal or greater benefit."*
>
> —*Napoleon Hill*

Know that you can free yourself from that scared person inside. When something disturbs you and the endless self-talk starts in your head, allow yourself some distance. Relax and turn away from the noise in your mind. You always have a choice. Either you lean into the noise, dramatize and emphasize it, or you turn away from it and create some space so it can pass by.

You can make every moment of your day a spiritual experience. Look at the reality of a situation from another angle, and then allow the stillness to set in. You might start seeing an opportunity instead of a problem.

What is the camera of your experience focusing on?

What I have learned most about focus

Over the years of learning to deal with my stress from within, one of my greatest lessons has been: Whatever you focus on is what you get, and what you concentrate on gets bigger.

> *"Whatever you hold in your mind on a consistent basis is exactly what you will experience in life."*
>
> —*Anthony Robbins*

I had never been taught this lesson when I was growing up, not at school and not at home. Since then I have learned that you create your reality with your focused thoughts. By now, most of us know this as the Law of Attraction. It was first described in the late 19th century and since then many authors have written about the effects of the Law of Attraction on health and other aspects of our lives. Louise Hay discusses it in her book "You Can Heal Your Life." If you are not familiar with this important law of life, I recommend strongly that you read about it in more detail. For further information, you will find some useful resources at the back of this book.

What you focus on, you will experience. What you focus on becomes your reality. Therefore, is it not worth directing your intention and attention on what you truly want and like, instead of concentrating on what you fear?

This Law of Attraction is very powerful. It works with small everyday things in life, such as wanting to find a parking space on a busy street, as well as with big things such as finding a job or regaining health. For me, it is like the Universe is continuously answering our loving requests. I always call them "miracles."

Story:

In the early years of my coaching, I had a client who was not able to get pregnant. Everywhere she looked, she saw women with a big tummy or with a pram. She focused on these women with the thought that they had what she wanted and that she could not get pregnant. Her energy around this was jealousy directed toward the pregnant women and fear that she, herself, would never bear a child. Her focus was clearly on "not being able to get pregnant." This state of mind gave her so much stress, and it eventually became a source of chronic stress when her negative wish became more and more of an obsession, especially when her doctors told her that there was no medical reason for her not to get pregnant. Finally, when she realized how negative her focus was, she began to change it. She began to approach the scene of pregnant women with a positive focus. How grateful she was for all the newborns she met, how abundant the Universe was and how happy she felt that she, too, could become a mother. Within four months, she became pregnant and is now a very happy mom.

Perhaps you have heard how parents who could not get pregnant some-times adopt a child and then get pregnant naturally, "out of the blue"? In these cases, their focus had changed completely from "what they could not have" and all the negativity associated with this, to what was natural for them.

Now that we have realized how important it is to choose our focus carefully because it determines our reality, let's take a look at the specific thoughts "you" focus on.

Choosing your thoughts

"The greatest weapon against stress is our ability to choose one thought over the other."

—*William James*

Do you know that you have around 60,000 thoughts going through your head every day? Bob Proctor, Paul Martinelli, and Christian Simpson, all great leaders in the field of thinking patterns, amazed me when I first heard them talking about such figures. Knowing what your focus actually does, can you see that it is worth your while to consciously choose empowering thoughts instead of disempowering ones, starting from today?

We cannot control the thoughts that bubble up in our minds, but we can choose the thoughts we dwell on and the ones we actively put into our minds. So "re-mind" your thoughts. Actively imprint images of faith, joy and expectancy into your mind. You have the power; you have the authority. Choose your focus. Take ownership, grab it!

When I ask people in my workshops or coaching clients to give an honest percentage of how many negative thoughts they have versus positive ones, their answers range from 50% to 99%.

Examples:

Julie, a primary teacher, said that during the busy, stressful weeks in the winter semester, she could hardly cope with all the extra work she had to do at school. When she estimated that 95% of her thoughts were negative, she was not exaggerating. During the winter holidays, she thought it would be much less but only noticed a 10% difference. She realized that her negative thinking pattern was seriously engrained.

Alan, a bank manager who participated in a six-week workshop of mine, was amazed at how many negative thoughts he had when he consciously listened to his inner talk. His estimated 90% negativity was reflected in every aspect of his life, and it was hard for him to find joy in anything he did. It was interesting to see how that percentage changed during the workshop and he decided to do a one-on-one coaching program with me to take it even further, realizing the impact this one change in thinking had on his life.

Anyone who is experiencing chronic stress will confirm that the normal daily rate of negative thoughts is high, averaging around 80%. This may seem exaggerated to you, but I suggest that you pay attention to your rate of negative views and ideas for one day or even just an hour. Check it out for yourself. What is your negativity rate?

However, do not judge yourself for your proportion of negative thoughts if, indeed, you are having more than you expected. That is simply the way it is for you now. Accept it, and look at it from a place of empathy.

Decide to start examining the focus of your mind from now on. When you first do this, the internal shift will make you aware of what is going on inside of you. Only then can you start to alter it since the only change you can make is within you—an internal change, not an external one.

Many people are living from the outside inward. In fact, we are all programmed not to think! Instead, we are programmed to believe we have to look outside of ourselves to find the answers we need to "solve" everything, including resolving stress. However, the answers are not outside of us. The answers all reside within us! If you start thinking with intention and focus, your inner world will be so much clearer and all the fog and mist will disappear.

Breaking the cycle of negative thoughts

Anthony "Tony" Robbins, one of my role models in personal development and an inspiring motivational speaker, is a master of focus and intentional thinking. He explains how logical it is that we dwell on so many negative thoughts since we ask our brain so many negative questions. He teaches us that the brain is trained to look for the answers (thoughts) to the questions we ask. Example: When we ask ourselves: Why is this happening to me? Why am I so fat? How could he do this to me? Of course, you will find answers like: I am such a loser, I do not deserve better, I have no self-discipline, I always have bad luck, etc.

When you ask yourself a positive question, there is an immediate shift in your thinking, your brain goes searching for a positive answer or thought and you get on a train of positive focus. Example: How can I solve this? What can I say to get his attention? Which step can I take to start taking care of my body? Can you feel the answers that are coming up? Can you feel the search for solutions and positive thoughts? By changing your focus and asking yourself a positive question, you immediately shift your "state" of being.

Your state of being is the way you feel. Is that not our main goal when we are stressed: to change our "state"?

Master your state of being, be aware of your mind–body connection

Your state refers to the state of your emotions. Earlier in this book I said that the most basic emotion responsible for chronic stress is fear. Specifically, the fear of not being good enough. Let's take a brief look at the energy of fear and what it does to our bodies.

First of all, let us not forget that everything is energy or energetic in nature. Enough scientific evidence has shown over the past 50 years that the Universe consists of energy, and all matter is energy. Everything we can and cannot see and touch is energy, including our bodies. Your focus and your thoughts are also energetic. To help you examine your energy, ask yourself this question:

☐ *Do I spend the majority of my time in an energy of fear or an energy of love?*

As you can see in Table 1 below, we can categorize all thoughts and emotions under two basic energies: love versus fear. You can fill in your answers in the left or the right columns. One thing is sure, most of us who are suffering from chronic stress, have found ourselves to be in the left column, which represents the energy of fear, negativity and scarcity.

FEAR	LOVE
Anger	Forgiveness
Anxiety	Peace
Shame	Hope
Blame	Optimism
Guilt	Gratitude
Frustration	Joy
Worry	Satisfaction
Resentment	Affection
. . .	. . .
. . .	. . .
Distrust	Trust, Confidence
Disease	Ease, Health
No-Energy	Yes-Energy
Contraction	Expansion

Table 1

When you look at Table 1, you can see how the strong energy of love leads to sincere "trust" and "ease." At the same time, please realize that the energy of fear can put you in a very "distrustful" vibration, which may cause you to feel uneasy, and may eventually induce "dis-ease." I know from experience that this is a dangerous place to be. If you or anyone has consistent negative emotions, it can put you into a no-energy state and bring your whole body into contraction instead of expansion. Now you can clearly understand that your everyday focus, the thoughts you give attention to, have an impact on your body's state and composition.

The idea that our thoughts, feelings, attitudes and beliefs can affect our biology and our bodies either positively or negatively has been studied for many years. This is called "the mind-body connection." Over the past 20 years, mind-body medicine has evolved, and more and more current therapies and healing arts arise from that philosophy. Mind-body therapies are helpful in managing diseases like arthritis, heart disease, chronic pain conditions and much more.

To explain the mind-body connection in a simplified way, Deepak Chopra states that from the brain's perspective, there are only two kinds of input, positive and negative. Positive experiences lead to increase well-being and health. Negative input leads to decreased well-being and high risk for disease. By activating the mind-body connection, positive focus like gratitude can shift hostility, stress and depression into positive psychological states such as compassion and empathy. A powerful, optimistic input of thoughts enhances your whole physical and psychological well-being.

I sincerely believe that there is no insight more powerful than this when we want to shift out of chronic stress.

Our thoughts affect our body. Even more so, our thinking can transform it. Therefore, you have a choice. Either you focus on your energy of love and go for a healthy mind, body and spirit, or you can choose to dwell on thoughts of fear, doubt and shame. . .which typically ends up in disease. Again, it is your choice of focus that will make the difference.

The Law of Attraction, which states that a focus on positive or negative thoughts will bring positive or negative experiences into your life, works at its best when you combine the focus on thoughts with the feelings and states that go with them. The energy you create from concentrating thoughts and feelings cannot do otherwise than to return to you in a positive or negative way. It is up to each one of us to decide where to place our focus—our thoughts and feelings.

For more information on The Law of Attraction and the Mind-Body Connection, please see the "Resources" section at the back of this book.

Just changing your focus from negative to positive is not always enough. We need to stop judging things to be good or wrong and step into the neutral field of feelings and needs. I will elaborate on this in the next chapter.

Exercise 1:

The 24-hour mental diet:

Decide to choose only positive thoughts for the next 24 hours. Every time you catch yourself in a negative focus, be aware, change it by thinking of something you are grateful for and continue your positive stride. You can check in with yourself about how often your unconscious thought patterns take you almost automatically back to your negative thinking. But, if you are aware of it, you can change it. And if you can do this for one day, you can do this for seven days and more.

Start with 24 hours and notice what happens.

Exercise 2:
Meditation with focus:

Find a quiet place to sit where you will not be disturbed, anywhere you want and feel close to yourself. Close your eyes and keep your hands loosely on your lap. Breathe deeply with your tummy for a minute, and feel a peace coming over you.

Choose to focus on a word that gives you peace, for example, "breathe" or "peace" or "calm" or a mantra such as "ohm." While you continue to breathe deeply, repeat the word regularly to yourself. Notice the thoughts that are going through your mind, but do not pay attention to them. Just stay centered on your breathing, repeating the word.

Do this for about 10 minutes if you can and stay relaxed after that for a few minutes before returning to your daily activities.

Exercise 3:
Your summary:

Write down your summary of this chapter, of what it means to you to choose your focus. What have you picked up from this chapter that is new to you? By writing these things down in your own words, you will integrate it better. I even advise you to explain it to the people you live with or your friends. The more you express your view on this or what you have learned from it, the more you will master it.

Remember to celebrate!

What exactly can you celebrate today? And how are you going to do that?
Enjoy this moment of acknowledgement and praise yourself.

Please go to my website **www.shiftingoutofchronicstress.com** and let me know how you are doing. I will celebrate with you every step along the way.

Notes

Notes

Step 4

CHAPTER 7

Being Aware of Your Words

"Words are, in my not-so-humble opinion, our most inexhaustible source of magic we have, capable of both inflicting injury and remedying it."

—Albus Dumbledore

*I*n this journey of dealing with stress from the inside out, you have decided to take responsibility for your own circumstances and stress. You have also chosen to be honest and authentic with yourself, thus uncovering your real basic fears and beliefs. The acknowledgement of those will tell you where your real work needs to be done.

In Chapter 6, you also learned the importance of choosing and changing your focus and thoughts. In this chapter, we address our awareness of the words we say to ourselves and others, as they too reflect our inner state of stress and anxiety. If we choose your words wisely, we will feel a shift in energy and will experience the emergence of freedom, balance and inner peace.

Words are a powerful creative energy

When I started my personal path of development, of taking away each layer that covered the unique "me," I was quickly thrown into the world of positive thinking and the Law of Attraction. You are what you think, for sure. That is why the previous chapter on focus precedes this one. And I sincerely worked hard on my "thinking," and on changing my pattern of negative perceptions and focus that contributed so much to my stress and illness. And it worked!

At the same time, it was often frustrating for me to change those patterns, as my thoughts came over me like waves. My mental control sometimes slipped away as it rolled in as a "tsunami" of sentences through the voice in my head. So, when I grasped the concept of being aware of each word, not to think as much in thoughts but in "words," this whole practice became easier for me. I felt as though I could manage each word in my head better than the whole "thought." It all made so much more sense to me.

As a child, we learn a language to use words as symbols to express ourselves and to be able to get our messages across to others. We learn to communicate and connect with others through these words so people can understand us and we can understand them. Through that process, we learn to use these symbols to communicate with our own selves and we develop an ongoing conversation within us.

Similar to the metaphor we used in the first step on responsibility, Don Miguel Ruiz describes in his bestseller, *The Four Agreements*, how we can compare our words with a paintbrush or pencil and compare our lives with a canvas. It is totally up to us which painting (life) we are going to create, a living hell or heaven on earth. What are you going to express with your paintbrush? What you paint in your life and how it will turn out on the canvas depends on how you use your words. That is how powerful the creation of each word is. You can create the story you want. The story of "you."

As we have already learned in the previous chapter, everything in this visible and invisible world is energy—the computer I am typing on, the glass of water next to me, my own body, and the sun shining outside here in Spain where I am writing. So are your words that you express to yourself and to others. Do not underestimate their power as they totally shape your world.

"You can change your world by changing your words."

—*Joel Osteen*

Each word has a powerful force, an energy, because it comes with an intention. Every word can reproduce an image, an idea, a feeling or an entire story in your imagination. Thus, you set a vibration in motion that causes an effect, and it has a creative power that most of us ignore. We recognize the reality of things in our world and the greater Universe. We re-create that reality with our words and our interpretation.

So the question you can ask yourself is:

What intention do I have with the words I want to say?

☐ *Am I using words of love or words of fear?*

☐ *Am I creating a colorful, beautiful painting or a dark pessimistic one?*

Being able to use whatever words we choose can be the greatest gift when we use them in the direction of truth and love for ourselves. But the words we choose can also be the greatest poison if we use them against others and thus, against ourselves. Remember how Hitler transformed a big part of the world into a hell by using a few words. Compare that to the Dalai Lama who creates peace wherever he goes. How we express ourselves creates our circumstances.

Question:

☐ *When you have a difficult situation or are challenged by someone, do you use words to create even more drama, fear and resistance or do you speak words of hope, gratitude, compassion and love?*

With our words, we create our own story. That story becomes our truth, our own reality. Since our childhood we have heard how other people form opinions of others and express their points of view. Therefore, we have adopted those ideas and programmed ourselves to express our judgement on people and things. What we need to be aware of is that they are just our "opinions" of others, they are not the real truth (remember the truth behind beliefs). So when you use your words, remind yourself, where possible, to speak from a place of authenticity, without faking, judging or wanting to be right. Know that misuse of your words has such destructive power that it can destroy everything around you as well as yourself.

Let's look at two different ways in which we use words. Firstly, there's our inner dialogue when we talk to ourselves in our heads, which forms our inner world (and interprets our outer world). Secondly, there's our outer dialogue, consisting of how we use the words we know to express ourselves and communicate with others. These words cause an effect, either an energy of love or an energy of fear.

Our inner dialogue

You communicate more with yourself than with any other person. In your inner world, you'd have this voice in your head that almost never shuts up. As such, you better be your own best friend instead of your own worst enemy since that voice determines how you talk to yourself.

Most of us who are dealing with chronic stress are sabotaging ourselves. We repeat over and over that we are not good enough, not worthy, and without hesitation we speak words of judgement, guilt and shame. We relive the drama outside of us over and over again in our heads.

Our inner critic can be so dominating, judging everything we see and hear. He/she never stops as he/she has been a part of our indoctrination process from the time we were born. Remember the judge and the victim who rule our world? It does not have to be like that. You can ask yourself if what they say is really the truth.

Questions:

- [ ] *Which words do you say to yourself when you feel anxious, weak, frustrated, angry, tired or exhausted?*
- [ ] *Is it really true that you are not good enough, too fat or too old?*
- [ ] *Is it really true that you don't deserve love and that you are not worthy of love?*
- [ ] *Is that just because you believe the distorted thoughts in your head about the world telling you how you "should" be, instead of just being who you were born to be?*

Remember Step 2 (Chapter 5) in this process about your "beliefs." Our inner critic knows those beliefs too well and will expect us to live by them.

The standards and expectations that you subject yourself to determine the extent of your stress level! Do these expectations and opinions come from others, or society, or are they authentically yours?

Examples:

Did you choose your profession based on the opinion of others? Are you feeling resistance in your inner dialogue when you are at work? How do you speak about your work, if you are not in a place that you like to be?

Are you living a lifestyle that meets the standards of others but that you actually cannot afford, resulting in your inner talk reflecting your unworthiness and your dishonesty—all of which causes you major stress?

Whatever you say to yourself, listen! Listen to each word you feed to your mind because it has a huge impact on how you feel and your level of stress.

After months, even years into my conscious journey of healing myself from within, I never realized how much power and influence my inner dialogue had over my emotions, my state of being, my actions and therefore my outer world. Yes, I had worked on positive thinking and the power of thought, but I never considered the power of "every word" I said to myself. Gaining that awareness created a big shift for me. From that moment onward, I concentrated on the words of the voice that was talking inside my head all day long and all night long. Our inner dialogue is even gloomier when we lay in the dark, awake, anxious and worrying and unable to fall asleep.

It was frightening to discover how destructive my own words were. That was a turning point for me.

I was confronted by the knowledge that this voice was doing everything possible to keep me ill, to keep me down and low in the place of darkness where I found myself. I realized how self-destructive my own words were months before I became ill. There was no happy vocabulary in my head. More than anything else, I was often complaining and judging myself. I hardly ever said anything nice to myself in the months of financial struggle and chronic anxiety.

It is not surprising that this ongoing pattern resulted in an illness. Remember the list of two different energies in the previous chapter, love and fear, and their consequences? I was truly creating my own disease with distrust and fear and worry. My body went into complete contraction and then it shut down.

I have done the following exercise for months while working on my own self-healing process. It is the only way to become aware of the exact inner dialogue that you are playing in your head so that you can finally change it. Of course I had and still have my ups and downs, but overall my inner dialogue has less and less control over me. Step by step, I took conscious control over the tyrant in my head. Slowly but surely, I learned to be more impeccable with my words. In the beginning I did it minute-by-minute without condemning myself if it did not work well. I accepted it and tried again. I cannot tell you how much of a positive difference that has made in the circumstances of my daily life. I found myself bathing in a completely different field of energy. I felt so much lighter and I felt the love for myself. That shift can have an impact on every aspect of one's life.

Exercise 1:

Journaling

Please keep a little journal with you and write down the answers to the following questions. Reading your answers will make the exercise even more powerful and confronting.

- *What are you saying to yourself all day long, when you are looking in the mirror in the morning or when you are driving your car?*
- *When a stressful situation happens to you, or when circumstances occur that you do not like or that are hurting you, how are you talking about it in your head?*
- *What is your inner critic telling you?*

Just notice and become aware of your voice.

Do you have the voice of a judge within you, who is constantly convincing you that you are not "being" enough, "having" enough, "doing" enough? Is the judge using words like idiot, stupid, fat, angry, worry, bad, no way, should, never, etc. to punish you for a mistake you made a while ago and still making you pay for it now?

Or do you have the voice of the victim within you, blaming others, telling you it has nothing to do with you, that "poor me" is not responsible for anything that happens in your life? Maybe you are telling yourself that this is just the way it is and that nobody can change it. Is that true?

Listen to every word that you say to yourself. Concentrate and be aware of each word you say regarding your stress or the current circumstances in your life. This is a very important exercise. As explained in Step 2 (Chapter 5), "Examining Your Truth with Honesty," it is exceptionally important to check your beliefs. This exercise is equally important so that you can be aware of every word, which can teach you so much about yourself. Once we are aware, we can change our conversation with ourselves because that conversation creates our results.

Master in "dream building," coach and motivational speaker Mary Morrissey asks us to change the channel we are watching inside our heads. If you are only watching CNN, for example, the world news with its coverage of disasters and negativity is what you will see in your world, and you will not experience romance or music, only a sense of fear and drama. So change your channel. How about watching the Discovery channel instead where you can see and speak about nature's abundance and joy? Then you will experience exactly that.

Does that mean you need to "fake" your positivity? Some say: "Fake it until you make it." I don't agree. Sometimes I allow myself a few minutes to shout it out against a tree or hit a cushion against the wall when I am really upset, frustrated or hurt. I believe there is no use in suppressing those emotions or pretending they are not there. I allow my emotions to come out, even sometimes by writing them down. But then, very consciously, I shift, I switch and I use words of hope or gratitude to see the big picture and create a better place for myself.

I hope you understand even better now how your inner world creates your outer world.

Our outer dialogue

Now that you begin to grasp why our communication with ourselves is vitally important in shifting out of stress, let us look at how this applies to our communication with others.

– How we "tell our story" to others –

I remember so well the last months before I got sick, in fact, years before for that matter. I remember especially how I was telling my story, how I was using negative words to describe any situation in my life. Whether I was talking about our finances, about our kids at school or about all the work that still needed to be done that day, I talked in a negative or pessimistic way. I realized, only a short while into my inner journey, that I created more and more stress in my body and mind by using that negativity in my wording. When people asked me how I was doing, I was either dishonest, putting up a fake smile, while coming from a negative state inside. Or I was overloading my answers with words of complaint, judgement and darkness. I never understood at that time that I kept on emphasizing the negativity in my life by repeating it over and over again and that I was seriously harming my mind, my body and my spirit.

I hear it every single day in my practice. When we encounter a stressful situation, we use words of negativity and drama to tell the story at its worst. We are so in the middle of the storm that we do not grasp that we make it into a hurricane by doing this. How can your circumstances change if you are using the same words every time you talk about something that bothers you?

We think that things around us need to change first before we can talk about them in a different way. The late Dr. Wayne Dyer, an American self-help author of numerous best-sellers and, for me, one of the biggest masters and motivational speakers in personal growth, said: "*If you change the way you look at things, the things you look at change.*" I can add to that: *If you change the way you talk about things, the things you talk about change.* This describes how the laws of the Universe work since everything, certainly our words, is a form of energy. And the energy you radiate comes back to you, always. "Like attracts like" says the Law of Attraction. So be aware of how you tell your story, because it is literally "your" story, "your" message, "your" life. You are the artist and you can create hell with your story just as easily as you can create heaven.

When you realize the enormous power you have every single second of every day to create your life story with your own words, you will surely start using words of hope, gratitude, joy, positivity and love. You will have an amazing feeling when you become aware of the importance of your words. You can use every word you speak with a special intention, and you can use the color of positivity in your message or your story. This will have a totally different effect and result in your life, because the Universe always listens. You are in constant creation.

– How we talk "about" others –

"Gossip kills three people: the one who speaks it, the one who listens and the one about whom it is spoken."

—Author unknown

Gossip is a serious virus in our society. It truly is. From early childhood we hear our family and people around us spreading their opinion about others and expressing their points of view. They gossip as if their truth is "the" truth, how they think you "should" be. They use words of judgement and criticism to make a statement. It makes them feel good to bring someone else down, since it justifies their own lack of purpose in life. Later on, we gossip too, as we consider it to be normal. We find it even amusing to judge others about their clothes, their looks, their character, their jobs, their circumstances and their lives. We don't understand the effect this may have on other people and neither do we grasp the effect it has on ourselves.

When we become aware of the power of the words we speak, we realize that gossip is poison and it comes back to us as a boomerang. The author George Bernard Shaw says: "*Judge and you will be judged.*" Your opinion is nothing other than your point of view, and it has nothing to do with another person. It has only to do with your reality, your perception of the truth, "your" truth.

What prevents us from speaking highly of everyone or not speaking at all?

Exercise 2:

"The 72-hour gossip diet"

Decide not to give your opinion about anything or anyone for 72 hours and see how that works for you. Notice how others around you give their opinion on everything and everyone. You may be surprised at how accustomed we are to gossiping.

Afterwards, I advise you to begin speaking about others in a very conscious manner. This will have a huge effect on your level of stress. You will feel so much more at peace within yourself when you turn off the judge.

Please note, however, that it is important for you not to judge anyone else when they are gossiping. Unfortunately, they do not know any better and will do the best they can within their own awareness. Just notice and do not judge others for it.

You can keep your distance from it or express yourself about your conscious journey with this book. They might have their opinions ready, but do not let that hurt you! You know why you are doing this and that is all that matters.

– How we talk "to" others –

Communication with others is about connection, not separation. We forget each day that communication consists of a two-way process of mutual understanding in which participants exchange information. It means to strive for a connection with one another. All too often, we also forget that we are two parties in a conversation and we talk too much about ourselves.

 Story:

A few weeks ago, I was walking in the main street of our hometown, when a friend of mine, Amy, passed me. She stopped and said hello and asked me how I was doing. I was only able to say two words before she started giving me a whole lecture on her life and how much she

was struggling while finding a new home. Although she had asked me how I was doing, she did not listen and did not give me the opportunity to answer her question. She was just into her own world with her own story, never reaching out for a connection with me. When she was finished, she told me she had to rush home and so she never heard more than two words of my story. I said goodbye and had a laugh within myself. No use in judging her and being grumpy because I could not tell her my story. No, it is just interesting to see and feel how absorbed people can be with their own truth.

Have you also been in that situation?

The best way to communicate with each other is from a place of mutual power, or mutual empowerment and respect, rather than from a place where one is able to overpower another by raising his voice or pointing fingers. When one person overpowers another, the other party will either go into powerlessness or try to overpower even more with more judgement and abusive words. The following paragraph explains this more in detail. See if you recognize this in your own life.

– *Being right or being happy?* –

Have you noticed the long discussions, and even fights we have, just to make another person admit that he/she was wrong and that we were right?

So often in conflicts, it is all about being "right." It often becomes a power struggle; it happens within our families, social and business relationships. Let us be honest, we have grown up in a dysfunctional society where being wrong is obviously a disgrace. As stated before in this book, we have been indoctrinated from the time we were born with the message that our own worthiness is dependent on being perfect. Because making mistakes often resulted in punishment, we will do anything to protect ourselves from being ashamed or viewed as a failure, as not being good enough compared to others. And so we do everything we can do to be better, smarter, fitter and stronger.

Being "right" in our conversations, with our words, comes from that repeated pattern. By being right, we feel good. By being right, we avoid punishment and so we feel more important and worthy than the other person. What we do not understand is that there is never a winner in this game. Everybody is losing. Punishment or reward, it is both the same game. It induces feelings of unworthiness and distances us from who we really are and from what we are born to do, which is namely to connect from the heart. The heart is our source and it comes from a place of unconditional love.

In Step 6 (Chapter 9), we will talk more about that aspect of self-love.

Exercise 3:
Question yourself:

When you feel you want to be right in a conversation, ask yourself these questions:

- *Why do I want to be right?*
- *What is in it for me?*
- *What triggers me so much that I want to go out of my way to prove that my opinion and my truth is "the" truth?*

– Connect from a place of empathy –

"I think we all have empathy. We may not have the courage to display it."

—*Maya Angelou*

During childhood, we never learned to sit back, to stop resisting and just listen with empathy to someone else's story and truth. We never learned to really connect. As a therapist and coach, I have learned to listen to people and communicate with them from a place of empathy.

However, it wasn't until I came into contact with Nonviolent Communication (NVC) that I have grasped the real essence of that long-learned lesson. NVC is a communication process that helps people exchange the information necessary to resolve conflicts and differences peacefully. The process, introduced by psychologist Marshall Rosenberg, made me realize that we are made to connect in this world from a place of "natural giving." "To receive with grace may be the greatest gift," Rosenberg says.

In the NVC concept, we can only achieve this if we learn the language of the giraffe (the animal with the largest heart), instead of the dominant language in our society, the language of the jackal. The giraffe does not use any words of judgement, he observes the behavior of the person without evaluation. As jackals, we are trained to judge, to speak our opinion of a person or situation and not the fact itself.

Being able to listen to the needs of others or expressing our own feelings and needs to people, without judging them, is extremely powerful. Anything anyone says is actually an expression of a need that they have. All needs are universal as we are all created from the same energy. As the writer and lecturer Dale Carnegie explains in his work on self-improvement, we all have a basic need to be important for someone else. People around us have a need to be heard as each one of us craves acceptance, approval and importance.

However, it is imperative to realize that we are not responsible for the feelings and the needs of others. I can be compassionate but I do not need to look for an advice or a solution. Just being empathic, completely present and all ears, can be transforming for the other person.

If the concept of connecting via nonviolent communication appeals to you, I highly advise you to contact me or to enroll in a basic weekend course on NVC in your region. You could also read one of Marshall Rosenberg's books, such as *Living Nonviolent Communication* or *We Can Work It Out: Resolving Conflicts Peacefully and Powerfully*. The principles of nonviolent communication have given me such powerful insights that have helped me to communicate better with myself and others. Today I still continue to improve myself through trainings with international master trainers. Some of these people are committed to teaching these principles in schools and they show educators and children how to unlearn the way they have been taught to communicate. What a wonderful initiative as it leads to amazing results inside and outside the classroom.

Every training I receive within this concept makes me more aware of the power of my words. My intention is to become a more conscious grandmother to my future grandchildren, than I was a mother to my children. At the same time, it gives me the opportunity to teach these basic principles in my workshops and to intensify my empathy sessions with clients, which is nothing other than applying the "natural giving" that I have been born with, as were you.

– How we talk "to our loved ones" –

Speaking of being a mother and a grandmother, let us not forget to observe how we talk to our partners and our children and grandchildren. Write down the answer to this question:

☐ *How do you talk to the people you love the most?*

Notice and become aware of how you speak to your loved ones.

Of course, I am the first one to admit that when I was so stressed out, I always made those closest to me suffer the most, both consciously and unconsciously. My clients tell me every day how they are used to judging, commanding, hurting and criticizing their loved ones with their words. We are brought up that way. Only rarely do we use words to give compliments, confirmation, gratitude and love. Instead, we complain, nag and look at the things that do not exist and at what is wrong, instead of looking at what is and what is ok. The more stressed we are, the worse it can get. We can be super reactive, raise our voices and bark like a dog, only to realize that it strains and frustrates us even more.

There is no excuse for this kind of communication. It is imperative to listen to yourself, every word you say, whether you are stressed or not. I know how hard it is, believe me. I know how difficult it is to see the positive when you are suffering, tired or exhausted. But still, there is no excuse.

Be aware of your words, every day, time and again. Make the commitment to be impeccable with your words. It is one of the most profound changes anyone can make to help themselves shift out of chronic stress, no matter how bad their situation may seem.

Exercise 4:
Set your intention

Intention is a powerful tool for transformation. Every morning when you wake up, set an intention for yourself. Take a moment and ask yourself:

"What would I like to manifest in my life today?"

Use your focus and words accordingly during the day and enjoy living with intention! You will experience miracles.

Exercise 5:
Your summary:

Write down a summary of this chapter, of what it means to you to be aware of your words. What have you understood from this chapter? What have you learned about yourself?

By writing it down in your own words, you will integrate it better. I even advise you to explain it to the people you live with or to your friends. The more you express your own view on this or what you have learned from it, the more you will master it.

♡ Remember to celebrate!

What exactly can you celebrate today? And how are you going to do that? Enjoy this moment of acknowledgement and praise yourself.

Please go to my website **www.shiftingoutofchronicstress.com** and let me know how you are doing. I will celebrate with you every step along the way.

Notes

Notes

CHAPTER 8

Developing New Empowering Habits, Unlearning Disempowering Ones

"We are what we repeatedly do"

—Aristotle

To dissolve the stress and fears in your life, you need to look at the habits and rituals you perform that disempower your thinking, speaking and acting. There is nothing as powerful as repetition when it comes to learning or changing anything in your life. This also counts for shifting out of chronic stress. We have already gone over a few of these habits in the previous chapters but some will require your special attention.

"If you do what you have always done, you will get what you have always gotten."

—Anthony Robbins

Because we have been programmed by others and also by ourselves, most of our behavior happens unconsciously, resulting in our habits and patterns. We are often unaware that we still have some of our old habits while in fact, most of the time, they are still taking place unconsciously. To change your results, you need to consciously change your habits through awareness and repetition. In my life, until today, the undoing of these patterns has provided me with more energy and freedom and certainly more inner peace and balance.

Author and public speaker Dr. Deepak Chopra says that it is difficult to change habits because they become bundles of conditioned reflexes that are constantly being triggered by people and circumstances into predicted outcomes of behavior. He has found that the only way out of those conditioned responses is through education.

In this chapter, it is my intention to educate you regarding the habits that consistently induce your fear of "not being (good) enough." In doing so, you will become "aware" of them, and that is the start of real change.

Breaking a habit can seem very difficult and can make you feel uncomfortable. Author Charles Duhigg explains in his book *The Power of Habit* that habitual behaviors are traced to a part of the brain called the "basal ganglia." This is a portion of the brain associated with emotions, patterns and memories. Decisions, on the other hand, are made in the "prefrontal cortex," a completely different area of the brain.

When a certain behavior becomes a habit, we function on autopilot, not using any decision-making skills. Therefore, to break habits and acquire new ones, we not only need to actively make new decisions, but we must correct our feelings as well, since the new habits often "feel" wrong. This is because the brain will resist any change in favor of what it has been programmed to do.

To overcome this, simply embrace the wrongness that you feel and accept that it will take a while before the new habit will begin to feel right, good or natural. Learn to discipline yourself to adopt the new habit anyway.

The habit you need to master first to shift out of chronic stress:
– Develop self-discipline and perseverance –

The first thing I want you to grasp before unlearning any disempowering habit is the importance of self-discipline. Before anything else, self-discipline is a habit that must be installed in order to shift out of chronic stress once and for all.

"If you discipline yourself today, you'll enjoy your life tomorrow."

—*Vicky Hitzges*

The first traits of self-discipline are self-knowledge and self-awareness, which we have often addressed in earlier chapters of this book. Self-discipline is the ability to make yourself do things that you may not feel like doing with the intention of improving yourself. It is the one quality that promises you long-term fulfillment and happiness in every aspect of your life. It is an internalized behavior that requires repetition and practice in your daily life. It helps you to make healthy choices and decisions instead of emotional ones.

Please note again that it is imperative not to judge yourself when you cannot break a habit right away. Often it has nothing to do with willpower. We condemn ourselves so easily if something does not work immediately.

We very often misunderstand the power of habit and, therefore, judge ourselves or others for being incapable of breaking one.

I often see it in my practice and workshops when people start to grasp the concepts I work with. They want to apply them and then judge themselves harshly for not being able to change their habits instantly, even if these particular patterns were there for over 30 years. It does not work like that. Being aware of the habits is not enough. Continuous discipline and perseverance are needed to change them.

Story:

When Jane came to me for the first time, she told me she was close to a burn-out. She felt that every single action was too much. She could not shop for groceries anymore without feeling exhausted and could not perform her tasks at work without feeling overwhelmed and anxious. She worried about everything in her life and did not trust herself or anyone else. She was the only caretaker for her mother. She always volunteered to babysit her sister's children when needed. She took care of her neighbor's dog every day and was always the one to work extra hours when her boss asked her to. During our coaching sessions, we discovered that she had a pattern of always looking for external approval and confirmation from others. She became aware of the fact that she always said yes to people, no matter how overloaded her schedule was. No was not in her vocabulary.

Jane understood that her body and mind were giving her signals that she would now have to help herself first. She even knew that learning to say no was the only answer. After two weeks of trying, she was very upset, reporting to me that it was not working and that she was finding it too difficult to change her habits. Of course, changing her routines felt uncomfortable and, although she knew it was the best approach, she felt a high degree of resistance and fear. She needed to practice self-discipline and loving self-care to make the changes and persevere with the process. It took time, but she finally managed. After three months of coaching, she experienced such freedom and independence by being able to say yes or no when she wanted to. It became a natural habit for her to question first within herself if she was able and willing to help another person or not, without feeling guilty or needing to defend herself.

Whatever change you want to make in your life, it demands discipline, practice and perseverance to work through the resistance of your old pattern and to make the new habit feel natural to you. You will have ups and downs; there is no way around it. The key is to keep moving forward. When you have a set-back, acknowledge it and move on. Do not dwell on the emotions of guilt, anger or frustration, which will disempower your self-discipline. Forgive yourself and get back in the driver's seat as soon as possible.

"Remember that the price of discipline is always less than the pain of regret!"

—*Nido Qubein*

Now that you understand the power of self-discipline, you are ready to unlearn some draining habits that deplete you and are responsible for maintaining your stress level.

Unlearn the 6 following depleting and disempowering habits

1. Comparing yourself to others

One draining and stressful thing most of us do in life is compare ourselves to others and measure our lives within their parameters instead of our own. This keeps us from accepting of who we truly are.

In a society in which prestige, intelligence, speed, technology and outward appearances are highly valued, we become easily accustomed to comparing ourselves to others. In the classroom, we learned that because Mary received an A in math, she was smarter than Josephine, who received a B. We were taught to look at others and try to be as good as they were. We were rewarded for being the best and punished or judged for not performing as well as others.

We compare everything with everyone on a consistent basis, whether it is about our clothes, cars, jobs, homes, or anything else. It is ingrained in us from when we were young. We do it consciously, and even more so unconsciously.

Become aware of how you compare yourself to others. Although this may seem to be motivating in a certain way, in truth it is exceptionally stressful, much more so than we often want to admit.

This perpetual comparative tendency means that our attention and intention is directed outward, rather than within ourselves. It means we are busy all day long, every day, trying to have a bigger car, a bigger home, a better paid job, a more exotic holiday destination, and also trying to be smarter, better looking, richer. It means we are judging everyone, most of all ourselves.

How can one mind be at ease when it is constantly looking around and comparing? If our focus is always on the outside world, it is impossible for us to relax, to be grounded and to be our authentic self.

Story:

Marc, a father of two, had been raised by his father, who was in the army. He said that his father was always comparing him with his older brother, who was into sports and competitive as a child and later appeared to be smarter and brighter, allowing him to go to university. Marc had "only" done nursing school. He carried on about the stress in his life and it was clear that he was constantly comparing himself to other people. His father had done it when he was young and now, he did it to himself and did the same with his own children. Only through our sessions together did he realize that this pattern of comparing was causing him a huge amount of stress, suffering and the misguided shame of never being good enough and never having enough.

Watching how others live their lives is an underlying, invisible form of alertness that people live with, and it can cause a chronic state of stress. This watchfulness consumes your energy—wasted energy that you could instead save and spend on your own growth or that you could spend on helping someone else in need.

The question of "How am I compared to others?" is a question raised by the ego. When people grow up with shame and a comparison-based identity, they lose a sense of themselves and who they are, as well as of their self-worth and uniqueness.

Perhaps we think we don't compare anymore, we think that over the years we have become smarter, but the underlying ingrained pattern in our subconscious mind is often still doing it.

Exercise 1:
Question yourself:

Let us pause here for a moment. Ask yourself the following questions and write down the answers. Do yourself a favor and be honest with yourself.

- *Am I still comparing myself to others?*
- *With whom am I still competing? Anyone specific?*
- *In which area of my life do I still feel the need to compare?*
- *Why do I need to compare myself to anyone? What is in it for me?*

Become aware of your feelings and needs regarding this habit of comparison and acknowledge them.

Commit to yourself that you will not identify yourself through others and that you will stop judging yourself as being not good enough. Trust yourself as an individual and value your uniqueness.

In Step 6 (Chapter 9), the chapter on self-love, we will spend more time on how to look within and accept yourself exactly the way you are.

2. Taking things personally

Both as a youngster and as an adult, I used to take "everything" personally, whether someone commented on my clothing or shared an opinion on my tennis game or did not greet me in the street. It struck me like lightning. I would blush, feel anxious and even guilty.

To take things personally is a matter of not understanding how all of us live in our own worlds, in our own truths. Because nothing we say or do is related to anyone but ourselves. I will repeat that in another way: nothing anyone says or does is about "you," it is all about them.

Example:

When you see me wearing a red shirt and you tell me that that color does not suit me and that blue is a better color for me, what does that say about me and red? The answer is nothing. It only says what you think of how red suits me. Your opinion is not a fact, it is your point of view on the reality of me wearing red. It is your world, seen through your eyes, not through mine.

This may seem a ridiculous example, but you would be amazed how often we absorb the opinions and actions of others onto ourselves.

Most of the time, we take something personally because at some level we agree with whatever was said. We lack self-love, and are too dependent on the confirmation and approval of others, fearing rejection. Therefore, we take in what was said and let that rule our feelings.

In the example of the red shirt, if I believe myself that the color red does not really suit me, I will take it more personally than if I believe that red is my color and it makes my brown eyes shine. I will stand in my own truth and be indifferent to your remark, as it only reflects your opinion and not mine.

It is important to understand that nothing, and I repeat "no thing" (nothing) of what others say or do is about you. It only involves them, since they live in a different reality than yours. Whatever they think or feel about you and your world is their opinion, it is their perception, their reality.

The world they inhabit is created by the way they were programmed when they were young. They see you and the outside world through their own eyes, their perceptions and experience, which is completely different from yours.

Can you see the power in breaking the habit of taking things personally? You will stop absorbing someone else's poison and you will start trusting yourself again. Your envy, jealousy and anger will dissolve. Do not take anything personally.

Exercise 2:

Observe and write down

For the next 7 days, observe how people live in their own realities. Whatever they say or do, just observe and listen. Do not let it touch you in any way. Do not take it in. Repeat to yourself: "This is their point of view which gives me insight into their world but says nothing about me." See how that makes you feel. Write it down.

3. Doubting yourself and your decisions

If you often doubt yourself, you probably have a hard time making decisions. Doubt, after all, is a lack of trust. When you cannot make up your mind, you are not trusting yourself.

In my own life, I feel that doubting myself was a difficult habit to undo. I am sure it all stems from judgements that came my way when I was making wrong decisions in my youth. I remember my decisions were often overruled by my parents or other authority figures like teachers. I often felt that I was not good enough, and questioned whether or not I had done the "right" thing. I also doubted my decision-making ability–and even my daily choices. For example, when I was in a restaurant, I never knew what to choose from the menu, the chicken salad or the vegetarian platter? What are the others having?

Now, I don't do that anymore. I go for what I like most and what I feel like at that moment. I listen to myself, not to anyone else. I finally rely on myself and thus trust my decisions.

When you are hesitant and indecisive, when you have no fertile ground in your mind, you cannot expect beautiful seeds to take root and grow. Doubt and indecision clutter your mind as all the possible outcomes accumulate. We all know what clutter can do in a house. . . it is overwhelming and confusing and makes us feel uncomfortable. To feel better, you need to clean up your cupboards, your garage and your basement so that you make room for the new things. Learning to trust yourself and your own decisions can be like cleaning the clutter of doubt and indecision from your mind.

Learn to make decisions from within, with conviction. Get the facts and listen to the advice of others, by all means, but make the right call based on your inner voice.

Story:

My youngest daughter could never make a decision on her own about which clothes or accessories to buy. I remember my eldest daughter telling me about shopping with her sister in New York City while they were on a birthday trip. They both love shopping in

New York because things are less expensive than in Europe. The youngest one saw a beautiful watch that she liked. She asked her sister what she thought about it, but one opinion still wasn't enough. Using her smart phone, she sent a photo of the watch to two of her friends, asking for their approval of her choice because she doubted her own preference so much. Now, a few years later, she is less dependent on approval but sometimes still doubts her own instincts. Since she is a highly sensitive person (remember "highly sensitive person" [HSP] from earlier in the book) she is so attuned to what other people may think and say. She is aware of this pattern and is working on changing it.

Listen to your own voice inside of you, your instincts, your intuition. It is telling you whether something is good for you or not. Allow yourself to be still and listen. Your inner self knows exactly what you really desire and require. You do not need the approval or advice of others. You have the best possible advisor within you, your inner voice.

4. Pleasing people

It has taken me a long time to understand that trying to please people is just a waste of time and energy. As a highly sensitive person, for as far back as I can remember, I used to do everything in my power to favor people. I felt and acted as if it was my job to do my best to help everyone around me so that they would accept me or confirm that I was OK. Of course, this meant that I was stressed and hurt when I did not receive the appreciation I was craving.

There is a solid difference between helping people from within and pleasing people. The need to please people is destructive and stressful because you are doing it to get their recognition, to get something back. You do it from a place of scarcity. Therefore, it is draining and will cost you loads of energy since you are looking for external approval. With some you might get it; with others, you might not. As we saw above in the subsection "Taking things personally," whether people like you or not has nothing to do with you. Instead it is better to please yourself, listen to your intuition or inner voice and act upon it, without expecting others to like you for it.

There is a great amount of wisdom in this because the same principle can be applied to "giving." When you give to please or to impress people, you will never experience as much pleasure or fulfilment as when you give from within, give from the heart. When you give, do it unconditionally, neither to please nor to get approval, reward or recognition.

Pleasing others is incredibly draining. Learn to say yes or no from within, and only when you feel it is legitimate. Do not be afraid that someone will love you less because you say no to them and yes to yourself.

5. Talking instead of listening

Working as a physiotherapist, I treated people with my hands for more than 12 hours a day. While being busy massaging or mobilizing my patients, I always felt the need to talk, as silence made me feel uncomfortable. Only later did I realize how much energy it takes to speak constantly, and to avoid silence. It is a habit I still feel popping up occasionally, mainly because we were all educated and trained to talk, rather than to listen. I am amazed that we think we have to speak to kill the silence. Silence is energy, and there is a message in the absence of words. It can say so much more than mere words if we just listen.

How little do we listen, even to the things another person is saying directly to us?

Remember the example of my talkative friend Amy in Chapter 6? After asking me how I was doing, she did not listen to my answer because she was so absorbed in her own story. People do not listen to each other anymore. They speak about themselves and they avoid silence. We are trained to express ourselves with words, even though we were given one mouth and two ears.

In the practice of coaching, it is important for the coach to listen and leave space for silence so the client can go within, to think or feel. It is imperative to take in each word and its energy, and to watch the client's body language. Why do we not do that in our face-to-face encounters in daily life?

Being empathic is so liberating, so energizing. You can empty yourself completely, and it costs you less energy than talking. In nonviolent communication, we spend days training our empathy muscle, just being completely present for the other person. If you feel the need to speak about yourself, or share your view or judgement, try to undo that habit. Start to listen, go into deeper connection with yourself and with the other person through listening.

Exercise 3:

Listen:

In the next conversation you have with one of your friends or loved ones, please choose to listen instead of talk. Ask more questions than ever before. Be interested in how the other person thinks and feels. Do not give your own opinion or advice, just be there for them this time. Use your two ears instead of your mouth. Write down how that feels and how the other person reacts.

6. Perpetual thinking, living in your head instead of feeling

We live in a society in which living in our heads is almost required to be able to keep up with the pace that is expected from us. How often do you use the words: "I *think* that . . ." We hardly ever say: "I *feel* that . . ." We think, think and think again. We make up dramas in our heads, make assumptions, and worry about everything. Would it not be nice to stop being rational and start being emotional?

Feeling rather than thinking is such a major challenge for sensitive people in this over-stimulating society, especially since we are born to "feel" but have cut ourselves completely off from this beautiful capacity. We reason about everything all day long until our heads are ready to explode, instead of going within to be in touch with our emotions. (See Chapter 3 Figure 4.)

Feeling your emotions will guide you to understand your own needs better as we saw in the previous chapter. Being in touch with your true core is what this work is all about.

Feeling is something I needed to learn all over again when I got sick. Yes, I felt every ache in my body but I could not sense what was right or wrong for me. I did not go within to "feel" what was really going on or whether something was the right thing for me to do or not. I would think and think and think again, not knowing what all those voices in my head wanted from me. Most of the time, we count on our knowledge, on what we know from our education, to make decisions, instead of counting on our inner wisdom, which we can only reach through "feeling." Going to your source for inspiration and guidance is the best you can do to make any decision in your life. Stop thinking and start feeling.

The experience of "feeling" might surprise you, as it might direct you toward things outside your comfort zone. Your source wants you to have your best life, to live an adventure, and not to get stuck in habits that keep you small and down.

Don't be surprised that if you really "feel" and you actually do what your inner voice tells you to do, you encounter real fear. In personal development we call this "the terror barrier." It is literally a barrier of fear that comes over you when you are taken out of your comfort zone. You see, your habits can keep you in your comfort zone day in and day out. You will not even notice it while living on autopilot. But when we live lives of passion and authenticity, we challenge ourselves believing that we can do whatever we pursue and live the way we choose. We step out of our comfort zone. Once we break the barrier, we feel alive, we feel free and we experience what life is all about. If you have ever done a "death ride," you know the feeling I am talking about that occurs just before you jump and that lingers on after the ride. You feel terror before you experience the total excitement and freedom of going through that barrier. You really get a kick out of it!

Exercise 4:
Feel your body

To begin to feel, we need to be silent and be aware of what is happening. Put this book down and breathe deeply into your belly for a minute, and feel a peace coming over you.

Relax and concentrate on your breathing. Go into your heart and feel it pounding in your chest.

- Can you feel the beat?
- Is your heart talking to you?
- Does it say something that you need to hear and feel?

Take your time. Feel and listen to find out whether your heart has something to tell you. If nothing comes up, that is fine, too. Just feel what happens within your rib cage. Or maybe another part of your body has something to say. Silence and going within ourselves gives us the possibility to feel life from within. Do it regularly. Do not take your body for granted. Do a regular check-up within your body to see how it feels.

Exercise 5:
Get out of your comfort zone

Write down something that you could do in the next week that will get you out of your comfort zone. Something you always wanted to do but never had the courage for. Something you have been procrastinating about or something that is on your bucket list and that you feel like taking on.

Go and do just that and let me know how it makes you feel.

Develop two wonderful habits to help you grow consistently
1. Love making mistakes

"Our greatest glory is not in never failing, but in rising every time we fall."

—*Confucius*

If there is one thing we are taught wrongly, it is to be afraid of making a mistake. From pre-primary education onward, our learning environment insists on doing things the right way or not doing them at all. We were wrongly judged for making errors and so we did everything in our ability to avoid making mistakes. If we did make one, we felt bad, wrong and less worthy.

As adults, we punish ourselves not once but far too often for making one tiny error. We go over it again and again in our heads, although it is over and done with.

Be honest with yourself, when did you learn the most in life? Probably when you did something the "wrong" way. So keep on making mistakes, it is the only way to grow. There is no wrong way of doing things, only "another" way.

"If you have not made a mistake today, you have not lived" is a sentence that I adore and often mention in my practice.

Note the following acronym:

FAIL = First Attempt In Learning

Some clients of mine have a fear of failing, so they do nothing. They are so scared to be criticized that they do not even try. They do not understand that by doing nothing, you fail and lose out in a much bigger way than by taking action. You only fall short when you quit or do nothing. People who take action and learn from their mistakes are growing, not failing. This brings us to the next empowering habit.

2. Always do the best you can

To always do the best you can is an essential habit that I want you to practice while shifting out of chronic stress. It contains a profound message. As we discussed earlier, awareness is the start of change but awareness alone is not sufficient. It is practice that makes the master! Whatever way you are living your life right now is the result of many years of practice so that it has become automatic.

Most of the chapters you have read until now have been asking you to shift out of your years of conditioning and start to pay attention. Becoming aware of your responsibility to yourself, your honesty within, your focus, your inner and outer dialogue and finally your disempowering habits has surely brought you to a place of change from within. But as we discussed in this chapter, it is the practice of these things that will make all the difference in your life and your stress level.

You can only "do" your best, and that is it. No more, no less. That includes the part of "doing" in which you take action. Often, I hear people say "Yes, I will try." Trying is not doing. Stop "trying," and just "do" it. Decide to take action and go for it, or else you might as well keep on trying forever.

However, the part about doing "your best" will change from moment to moment. For example, when you are feeling sick, your "best" will be different from when you are in good health. Giving your 100% is the norm. But when you are sick, you might only be able to give 60% of your ability. Doing the best you can is then giving 100% of that 60%.

To unlearn what you have learned for so many years and to replace your disempowering habits with new ones might be difficult but you will regain your personal power. It will be worth it. So, do the best you can, no excuses and no judging.

If you make a mistake, start over, keep practicing until your new habit takes root. You will slowly but surely transform yourself until one day, it will become more natural to do things the new way and it will eventually become a new "empowering" habit. This brings us to the core message of this book, which I explain in the next two chapters. Doing the best you can with all of these conscious steps to reduce chronic stress will make you feel free and light and authentic. You will be ready to accept and love yourself unconditionally and practice loving self-care every single day of your life.

Exercise 6:

Your summary:

Write down your summary of this chapter, including which habits you find disempowering for yourself and which ones you want to re-incorporate. Are there any disempowering habits that are not mentioned here that you would like to get rid of, or empowering ones that you would like to master?

What have you understood from this chapter? What have you learned about yourself?

By writing it down in your own words, you will integrate it better. I even advise you to explain it to the people you live with or to friends. The more you express your own view on this chapter or what you have learned from it, the more you will master it.

 Remember to celebrate!

What exactly can you celebrate today? And how are you going to do that? Enjoy this moment of acknowledgement and praise yourself.

Please go to my website **www.shiftingoutofchronicstress.com** and let me know how you are doing. I will celebrate with you every step along the way.

Notes

Notes

CHAPTER 9

Making Self-Love Your Source

"The most powerful relationship you will ever have is the relationship with yourself."

—Steve Maraboli

*N*ow we are coming to the core messages and teachings of this book as we reach Steps 6 and 7 (Chapters 9 and 10). Accomplishing these last two important steps will certainly shift you out of chronic stress for good. You are going to remind yourself who you were before the world told you how you "should" be. This step goes to the core of who you really are. Because therein lies the secret: loving and caring for yourself exactly the way you are, without any judgement. Choose to love yourself with all your flaws and imperfections so that your fear will disappear. Your chronic stress will dissolve because it cannot survive in an environment of loving self-care.

If you have not yet realized it, your relationship with yourself is the most valuable and most important relationship of your life. Because that one important connection determines how you show up in your relationship with anyone or anything else in this life. The quality of your connection with others is directly in proportion to the quality of your connection with yourself. The person you will spend the most time with in your life is "you." Every single day of your life, you wake up with yourself, and you go to sleep with yourself. Therefore, it is worth investing more in that relationship than in any other. It is imperative to take out all judgement, blame, and guilt. "You, Ltd." is the most important business you will ever run in your life. "*You are your best investment!*"

Each paragraph in this chapter brings you closer to loving yourself exactly the way you are and shows you how to do it.

Lovingly accept your flaws, shadows and weaknesses

"You do not need to complete yourself; you need to accept yourself completely."

—Louise Hay

We all have parts of ourselves that we prefer to hide, as we think of them as shortcomings or weaknesses. We feel ashamed of them, whether they are character flaws or physical deficiencies or weaknesses or any other type of flaw. The fact that we think we are not good enough can inspire us to feel ashamed and insecure. Often, it might even lead to self-destructive behavior, which we have seen before.

It is important to decide to look at our deficiencies and weaknesses with love and compassion and choose how we will live with them. Are we going to hide them or share them? Sharing them, of course, takes them out of the shadow and sets them into the light. When you expose yourself out there in the world, you will not feel ashamed; instead, you will be surprised how authenticity brings you strength and liberation.

Dr. Brené Brown, author and public speaker, talks about it in her work. She says that vulnerability is where your true power resides. Permit yourself that vulnerability because it is not only humbling, it is the birthplace of connection with yourself and the path to the feeling of worthiness.

Your shadows and flaws are part of your human nature. We all have them; they are not defects. On the contrary, they are parts of you that need special attention without hesitation. So stop hiding and stop lying to yourself. Be authentic in every aspect of your being.

Story:

A young woman, Ashley, came to see me feeling exhausted and overwhelmed. When she greeted me, she was looking down, her eyes hidden behind very thick glasses. She had a baby of nine months and had a lot on her mind. She said she needed help to cope with everything.

After agreeing to take responsibility for herself, we looked at what was really going on in her life. She revealed to me that she had a very serious handicap with her eyes and vision, which would deteriorate even more in the future, and she was so embarrassed about it that she was hiding her beautiful self behind it in every aspect of her life. She found herself unworthy, having always been judged by both of her parents since she was a small child. And her eye condition made everything worse, she said. We worked on the judging part so that she could begin to understand that she was also judging herself now for "not being (good) enough," mainly because of her eyes and her weight. By slowly accepting her eye condition, and looking at it from a different perspective, such as how it had made her stronger, she started to love herself.

When she finally valued her courage and perseverance enough to live a life as normal as possible, she even decided to invest in a beautiful pair of glasses. She is wearing a red pair now; she is shining, putting herself out there in the world. She has a new job and is taking care of her body with love and acceptance. She is very gentle and patient with herself. She has accepted her flaws along with her whole self. Her self-love has changed her life.

Former fashion model and inspirational speaker, Renée Airya shares her beautiful story about accepting herself, regardless of her flaws, in a very inspiring speech. She says at the end: "*True success lies in how we perceive ourselves. If you feel internally imprisoned, you will never feel free through any amount of money, any top job or any romantic relationship. The only way to experience freedom and inner peace is through the amount of love and acceptance you have toward yourself.*"

This is what my life's work is all about. To shift consciously out of chronic stress, you need to drop all judgement and practice self-love and self-care at your core.

Accept and love yourself, unconditionally

"To be beautiful means to be yourself. You don't need to be accepted by others. You need to accept yourself."

—*Thich Nhat Hanh*

When my clients and I have gone through a part of our coaching path together, I sometimes put them in front of the mirror to have a deep look into their own eyes and say: "I love you." I learned about this mirror work through Louise Hay's workshop and books. Because her philosophy worked miracles for myself, I often use it in my practice. Some clients cannot look into their own eyes; they are not used to looking at themselves with love as they judge themselves from the moment they look at their reflection. Some of them cannot love themselves yet, but are ready to say: "I accept you." Others finally, for the first time in their lives, can say those magic words softly or convincingly: "I do love you."

In my life, I taught my children to love themselves when they were in primary school. After brushing their teeth in the morning, I would encourage them to look consciously into their own eyes in the mirror and say those magic words. They loved it, and it gave them bright shiny eyes. Can you imagine the attitude and energy with which they went to school? They looked as though they could handle anything that came up and as if no one was going to stop them!

The most difficult part for adults is to say these words without conditions. That means loving yourself not only when you lose 10 pounds, not when you will have a new job, or not when there is more money in the bank. The key is to love yourself without any condition but with compassion. All of our self-condemning, such as finding ourselves too short, too tall, too heavy, or anything else, are just opinions. They are just points of view and it is imperative to know that these point of views were not there when you were born. Society shares its opinions and gives you images of how you "should" be and "should" look. And then, you interpret yourself and judge yourself according to everything that you know, according to what you have been led to believe. As you have gone through our first five steps of this powerful shifting process, you are ready now to see the true you, the core of you.

Exercise 1:
Accepting yourself

Stand in front of a mirror and look into your own eyes. What do you see? Can you say to yourself, "I accept you" or "I love you"?

Don't judge yourself if you cannot say it. Just come to this mirror regularly and just look in your eyes, even without saying anything. Just feel what comes up.

If you find this exercise ridiculous, or painful or impossible, it means something. Find out why this exercise is hard for you. What could you discover about yourself?

Exercise 2:
Affirmation

Choose an affirmation like: "I accept myself exactly the way I am." or "I love and accept myself every day in every way." Say your affirmation out loud as soon as you open your eyes in the morning and as many times as you can during the day. Just repeat it, relentlessly. You can even make it into a song and sing it out loud.

Self-love is not selfish

"It's not selfish to love yourself, take care of yourself, and to make your happiness a priority. It's necessary."

—Mandy Hale

So many times when I talk about self-love as a concept of basic health and wealth, whether it is in my workshops, or in coaching, or in conversations with friends and acquaintances, I get the remark: "But that is so selfish!" Is this not another proof of those judgements that we have integrated into our thinking about what is right and what is wrong? Thinking that everything we do for ourselves is motivated by our selfishness was something that I grew up with. Taking the biggest part of cake on the plate or standing first in line to jump on my favorite horse on the carousel, and having a strong self-esteem as a youngster was just not done. Instead, I was told that I had to be modest, and first always ask others what "they" wanted.

The self-love I am talking about here goes much deeper. When I explain to people what self-love means in "my" dictionary, they get it and see the unquestionable value in it.

Selfishness (egoism)	Self-love (healthy selfishness)	No self-love (altruism)
Always at the expense of others	Not at the expense of others	Never at the expense of others
Not at the expense of oneself	Not at the expense of oneself	Always at the expense of oneself

Table 2: Explaining self-love.

Self-love, as you can see in the table above, is a "healthy selfishness." When you look at the left column, you have selfishness, living from your ego, at the expense of others, and not caring for other people's needs.

The outer right column is the one of altruism, where we have no self-love and do everything for others at the expense and sacrifice of ourselves. We look for confirmation and approval outside of ourselves and do all we can for others while neglecting our own rights and needs. We are fulfilling only our duties in society, and not taking our rights into account.

In the middle, we see the self-love I am talking about. It is a philosophy of living out of love from within, pure and giving to ourselves and others. That means that self-love is not at the expense of ourselves, nor at the expense of others. It is the only way to live a balanced, fulfilling life.

I ask you to create "your new definition" of self-love and embrace it.

Loving yourself is not selfish, it is your birthright and even stronger, I dare to say: "It is your duty in this life to honor yourself with your unconditional love."

Loving yourself is your birthright

Loving yourself is your "birthright." Because you have been born, you are worthy of your love. Loving yourself is your spiritual path, it is the "source" of all that you are. It is the very energy from which all other energies like joy, freedom, passion, etc. originate. By loving yourself, you can express your true core, which is unconditional love.

Loving without condition is the only love that is pure, and it comes from the soul. Give it first to yourself, you have that right. Do not ask for permission.

Living out of love is experiencing love within so you can express it outwardly in a natural way. Does that not sound fantastic and beautiful to you? Can you imagine what this would do to you, to live from your source? To live in love and out of love, unconditionally? That is the key to a fulfilling life.

Exercise 3:
Be still and go within

Sit in a quiet place where you will not be disturbed. Maybe in the corner of your favorite room with a view, maybe outside in nature where you feel close to yourself alone, or anywhere you want where it is quiet and comfortable.

Close your eyes and keep your hands loosely on your lap, with your feet touching the ground. Breathe deeply into your belly for a minute, and feel a peace coming over you.

Take a few conscious breaths and go into your heart. Feel the beat, feel the love that radiates from there into your whole body. We talk about your love for your body, for you, for who and what you are. Love yourself, your mind, your body, your spirit and your soul. Listen and feel the deepness, the wholeness. This is about you, about feeling unconditional love for all that you are.

Stay like this and embrace yourself for a few minutes, until you feel ready to open your eyes again and continue your day.

You are born a miracle and a champion

Reflect for a moment on the journey that you had before you came into this world. Do you know that the odds of you being born at that exact moment in time with your parents are 1 out of 40 trillion? So you can only admit that you are a very special and unique Miracle with a capital M.

At the moment of your conception alone, 40 million sperm cells were battling to find that one tiny little egg, too small for the naked eye to see. Only one of these sperm cells won the race. They connected and melted together to form this little living cell, you. That is where your life started, against all odds. Acknowledge your uniqueness and champion skills. Whatever difficulties or obstacles you still have to conquer from today forward, none of them will be as tough as your winning battle at the time of your conception. Victory is yours, believe it and embrace it. You are a conqueror, a champion. Take on that starting point with admiration and pride toward yourself.

You are worthy and deserving

"Worthiness is not about who we should be or who we might be or who we could be. It's about who we are. Right now. Today. It's about waking up and believing, "I am enough."

—Dr. Brené Brown

Remember our basic fear of "not being (good) enough"? Well, I have news for you. The fact that you are born makes you worthy and makes you deserving of the best this life has to offer. You do not have to "do" anything to be worthy of love and life.

Just by "being" here, you deserve love. Not by acting right or wrong. Look at a newborn baby, how it is deserving of pure, unconditional love just by being here. It does not have to do the dishes, achieve a perfect score, or reach a deadline to be worthy. Each newborn baby is perfect as it is, with or without hair, with long or short legs, chubby or skinny. So instead of judging yourself time and time again at every occasion, feeding your inner critic, you need to go within and observe the miracle of "you." Because you are love, and that love cannot be destroyed, only forgotten.

"You, yourself, as much as anybody in this Universe deserve your love and affection."

—Buddha

Remind yourself of when you were a small child. Or look at a toddler. These small people respond to everyone and everything without any lack of self-worth. Honestly, that lack does not exist. They are completely authentic. They do not pretend to be what they are not. They are totally free to be what they are. They "own" their worthiness. They demand food when they are hungry, they say "no" when a request does not please them. They exercise their right to show how they feel and so on. But as the child begins to grow up, he is educated about what another person thinks he is doing wrong. The judgements, opinions and beliefs of others start to pressure him into installing the hidden, insidious problem within himself that he is not worthy. Not worthy of success, happiness, health, wealth and love.

In my honest opinion, this lack of self-worth ingrains itself silently and is the basis of all the suffering in our lives. Until finally, one day we become ill, have a crisis or something terrible happens to us. Then the tsunami hits us, as it hit me.

I thought I was OK, nothing more, nothing less. It wasn't until my illness and complete breakdown that I could see the underlying, unconscious pattern within me. I was always caring for others hoping to be deserving of love from myself and others. I never put my own care and needs first, nor did I invest in that loving relationship with myself.

Now I see that my EGO (Edging God Out) used my lack of self-worth consistently and forced me to look outside for fulfillment and love. I did everything in my power to find that confirmation of love and worthiness outside of me. I was loving, helping, pleasing, saving everybody while often also over-delivering, over-eating or over-exercising, never feeling the fulfillment from within. Always alert to someone else's needs, never listening to my own.

You cannot easily see the harm the ego does to you because it sometimes seems to protect you. Do not be fooled. Often, your ego keeps you down, showing you lots of ways in which you need to stay in your comfort zone to be like everyone else and not to be special. The ego resists change, progress, and growth of the soul. Yet, the ego is what it is and we need it in this society. We need our ego to deal with the practical aspects of life. The best way to function with "your ego" is to recognize it but not to identify yourself with it. Just be aware and notice your ego playing its part.

Surrender your old way of thinking, feeling, speaking and acting. Begin to truly feel worthy and deserving.

Make that decision

"Find yourself first, like yourself first, love yourself first. Friendship and love will naturally find you."

—*Mandy Hale*

Loving yourself and feeling worthy starts with a decision. A conscious choice that it is your right to be deserving and to love yourself, no matter what. You are here to live "your" life, not somebody else's. Not loving yourself is telling the Universe that you are unworthy of any positive outcome or love. Like attracts like says The Law of Attraction, and you will experience lack instead of abundance.

Decide to start loving yourself exactly for who you are, with the intention of healing your life, being happy from within and leading the life that you truly want. The conscious choice of loving yourself gives you an instant shift in energy. It will make you want to come alive. You will shine.

I love it when motivational speaker Lisa Nichols says: "*Turn your fear into fuel.*" Isn't that what it is all about? Decide that from now on you turn your fear of "not being good enough" into fuel to love and express exactly who you are, perfect and worthy of the best.

Time and time again, when people start to accept and love themselves, their whole energy changes. This obviously works like a boomerang as we have seen before in other chapters. The altered energy of that loving shift returns to us in a big way. Our results in life will be filled with love, too.

I always compare this phenomenon with a little stone that you throw into the water. It makes circles and creates change that goes on and on in a never-ending motion. Know that if you were only to make one change to transform the quality of your life, you might try to send a little love your way, or a lot.

Let the genius within you emerge

"*What lies behind us and what lies before us are tiny matters compared to what lies within us.*"

—*Ralph Waldo Emerson*

Spiritual guide Marianne Williamson talks about the human potential in an audio tape. It is important that we realize that we will never be discovered by anyone if we lack faith in ourselves. Because nobody is going to see in us what we do not see in ourselves. Stop waiting for the right movie producer and produce yourself. Be the star of your own movie. Practice being the person that you know you can be, even when no one is looking because the Universe is "always" looking.

It is a fact that we do not need to invent or discover ourselves, or our sense of meaning. We need to uncover ourselves and our meaning as they already reside within us. This is what we have been doing since the start of this journey during this 7 step process. We uncovered ourselves from all the indoctrination and limiting beliefs. We relinquished all of the obstacles, lies and illusions. Now it is time to let the genius within us emerge.

When we look at our children in preschool, we can see the unlimited obvious capacity for greatness. As mentioned earlier in this chapter, young children have a great sense of self-worthiness. But we cannot be blind to the fact that we and our society dampen and suppress their spirits. Our educational systems beat it out of them by pushing all children to meet some "normal" standard. So, we could instead teach those children to love and live in compassion and mainly keep them centered in their pure joy. Marianne Williamson says: "The world is not falling apart because children cannot spell, but because adults are not thinking for themselves. They are internally bound and un-free, and their genius is suppressed."

It is time to start sending love and compassion to yourself and change your opinion of yourself. Time to uncover your genius and experience the part of yourself that is immune to criticism and fearless toward a challenge. Never feel of less value than anyone else and simply express love. That is the key to expressing your genius.

Keep your promises to yourself and be gentle and patient with yourself

The love you have for yourself is directly reflected by the promises that you make and keep to yourself. When you easily break a promise to yourself, you show no commitment to your highest worth. Love yourself enough to keep your promises. Commit to being your own best partner, friend and lover and always have the highest, purest intention toward yourself. For good and for worse, in sickness and health, you can see this lifetime commitment as the most important agreement you will ever make.

At the same time, it is equally important to be mild, gentle and patient with yourself. In this book, we talk most about leaving all judgements behind to start a stress-free life. It is important to know that you cannot experience self-love if you are harsh on yourself, especially if you fall back into your old judging pattern. Be gentle and kind to yourself, be patient. This work toward a shift out of stress demands time and awareness. Just notice when you judge yourself again and move on. Keep in mind the habit of doing the best that you can, it certainly counts for loving yourself. When you catch yourself judging or victimizing, always be gentle and patient.

Give yourself the necessary "time" to go through this process. Do it all at your own pace. Time itself is a healing factor. Do not rush anything when it comes to changing or healing. "Shifting" out of chronic stress is a journey. If you give yourself the time and the space to shift, you will again experience miracles.

Connect to your inner child

"It is necessary to own and honour the child who we were in order to love the person who we are."

—Robert Burney, The Dance of the Wounded Souls.

By going within with the intention of sending love to your being, you automatically connect with your little "you." The undamaged you, your inner child, the one you were before someone else told you how you should be. You can connect with your core, the real you, your essence by going within. Why is it that we all love babies and toddlers so much? It is because of their innocence and their purity and their uncompromised inner beauty. What if you could get back to that part of you that is pure and perfect?

So much has been written about our inner child because it is the gateway to our higher self. So start nurturing and loving that little 4-year-old within you.

The only way to do that is to own that child's experience and to honor that child's feelings. This will release the energy of emotional grief that we are still carrying around. Although we mostly discuss the emotion of basic fear in this book, which implies all other feelings of anger, shame, guilt and grief, I do not want to underestimate the importance of feeling the grief that we experienced as a child. In doing so, we often recognize our most basic pain and can heal from there by giving ourselves unconditional love.

I experienced that firsthand by working with my inner child, who had covered up so many emotions related to surviving the loss of my little brother, my piano teacher and my favorite horse, all before my 10th birthday. So many feelings were suppressed and never found a way out. Instead, I convinced myself I was "fine," needing to save everyone else to be deserving.

Instead of "judging" feelings such as those described above, you need to witness and observe them. We were raised in an emotionally dishonest environment, where we were often taught that it was not OK to feel our emotions or to only allow some and not others. As a result, we judged and shamed ourselves and felt guilty. Therefore, we learned to control our emotions to survive.

Attempting to suppress them is dysfunctional. It does not work. We use food, drugs, cigarettes, TV and more to keep down the unaddressed and suppressed feelings. We do this instead of looking at the emotional wounds and allowing them to be there and embracing them. Emotions are energy. E-motion = energy in motion. Emotions are meant to flow, to move, not to be hidden. Unexpressed emotions remain inside of us and will manifest as illness if we do not let them out.

Feeling an emotion is absolutely fine as emotions of any kind are warning signals that want to protect us. Emotions make up who we are. Acknowledging the emotions that are there, will make the release of that energy easier. Until we do, we will keep on having that same dysfunctional relationship with ourselves and with others, experiencing chronic stress for sure.

Marshall Rosenberg, the founder of nonviolent communication, explains the emotional cause so well: Life is all about needs. Behind every feeling (positive or negative) that we have, there is a basic need. Either we mourn about one or more needs that are unfulfilled (negative feeling) or we celebrate the needs that are fulfilled (positive feeling). It is imperative to take the time to grieve for your wounds, as much as to embrace the joy of your fulfilled need. Either way, it is important to acknowledge that need from within and to welcome it instead of being at war with it.

Example:

My husband and I have been having a daily conversation about plans for a specific weekend. I can see that he is watching his TV at the same time. I feel disappointed and hurt because I have a need for respect and being heard when I talk. My needs are not being fulfilled, and that makes me feel that way. However, instead of going into conflict with him, I can go within to feel empathy for myself for the fact that my need for respect and being heard is so strong. I can maybe understand myself better now or work on it to see where else in my life that need for respect and being heard comes from. As a child, I needed so much to express myself and be heard in my own story. I remember that a lot was going on around the table at lunch or dinner. I was often punished for not eating all the food that was on my plate. We needed to eat and not to talk too much. I wanted to be heard when saying that I just had enough, but they punished me instead. This is just an example of where respect and being heard were unmet needs when I was a child. I do understand myself better now every time I am upset when someone does not listen to me when I talk.

In this part of the process, we can go back to that inner child and feel the needs it has today and the needs that have never been fulfilled.

Exercise 4:
Your basic needs

Do you recognize any of your needs that are not fulfilled in your daily life? What are those basic needs? Can you give empathy to yourself? Or do you want to take this further as you realize some of those needs were not fulfilled when you were a child? Take some time to write out those needs and look at them now with empathy and love for yourself.

The power of laughing, joy and fun

All too often, I see people who have lost their "joy." When I ask my clients what is fun in their lives, they have to dig deeply to come up with an answer.

You can look back at Figure 4 in Chapter 3, which illustrates the disconnection from ourselves as a result of chronic stress. Remember how highly sensitive people often get disconnected from their true core, their inner being, their inner child? They live in their heads and can no longer feel exactly what it is that they want. They do not know what gives them "joy" anymore. They are living on autopilot. See if you can identify what is "fun" for you.

Example:

I remember when I was on my healing journey, I had to find out for myself what did bring me joy in my life. It was such a difficult task because I was not enjoying anything at that time. I did not know what fun was for me anymore. I went back to my childhood and realized that I always loved to go on the swing. It made me feel as if I could fly. I decided to go back to swing in a playground close to our home, regularly, just to get back that blissful feeling. It brought life back into my core. I felt the same about drawing. I loved it. So that is what I did. I was feeding my inner being again by drawing. I am sure that this helped to bring about a shift in my process.

My clients experience that same shift when they go back to what they loved doing as a child. Remembering what gave you joy as a child brings you in touch with who you were before the world told you who you should be!

Even if you just start laughing more often during the day. Somebody told me once that kids laugh on average about 100 times a day while adults laugh about 4 times a day. Maybe it is time that you practice "smiling" and "laughing," it is excellent for your emotional and physical health. Try it out, it is worth it.

Instead of taking yourself always seriously, start laughing at yourself. Remember that being able to laugh at yourself is a sign of maturity!

Exercise 5:
Finding fun and joy

Find out for yourself what gives you real fun, pure childish joy. Then do just that as much as you can. See if it makes a difference in the way you feel.

Forgive yourself and others

It is time to let go of any animosity or registered grudge, of any resentment or anger. We think we hurt another person by holding them accountable, but all we do is hurt ourselves as it reflects itself inwardly. Like the South African leader Nelson Mandela says: "We drink the poison ourselves if we are unable to forgive."

Decide to let go of the hurting memories of the past that poison you. Allow the pain of the past to finally disappear through forgiveness; otherwise it can contribute to the development of serious health issues. Unreleased, unresolved past issues inevitably manifest themselves physically in the body. Research at John Hopkins University indicates that long-term unresolved resentment is a contributor to cancer. The fabulous movie, *The Cure*, reflects on all aspects of the mind-body connection. It is an extraordinary confirmation of what we talk about in this book. That it is all up to you. To shift out of chronic stress is up to each individual, up to "you."

To forgive yourself and to love yourself unconditionally have been proven to be fundamental to any healing or state of wellbeing. What we did in the past was because we did not know any better; most of us do things unconsciously. We do what we have learned to do, what we have been indoctrinated to do. Understand that it has become "un-conscious." We copy our parents as they copied theirs. Now it is time to let go of our judgements, guilt, resentment and shame. It has been proven that forgiveness will never fail to set you free.

Exercise 6:
Affirmation of forgiveness

The following affirmation of forgiveness comes from one of the additional videos of "The Cure." I include it here to give you a tool for everyday reading and your practice. You can start from today onward to forgive yourself and others for all judgements that we have talked about earlier in this process. It is exceptionally powerful and healing, no matter where you are in your life right now.

Affirmation of forgiveness:

I forgive all those who I feel may have harmed me.

I forgive my parents and those closest to me who may have treated me in ways I did not like.

I forgive everyone who I may believe has acted wrongly.

I especially forgive myself for anything I may ever have done that does not measure up to my values and beliefs.

I lovingly let go of judgements that are holding me back from enjoying life to its fullest.

As I learn to forgive, I open myself to a life of pure joy and happiness.

I find the greatest result when I lovingly forgive and accept myself as I am.

As I eliminate anger and resentment, the warmth of love circulates through my mind, my body and my world.

The energy that I would have used in being angry, I now release
to love.

I dismiss all tendencies to be angry, fearful and resentful.

In exchange, I am filled with love, faith and trust.

Develop an attitude of gratitude

"When you are grateful, fear disappears and abundance appears."

—Anthony Robbins

An attitude of gratitude is part of the basic self-love we need to have for ourselves. It is the most basic ingredient for inner peace. You will never be fulfilled if you cannot be grateful for who you are and for what is present in your life. The energy of gratitude is the strongest positive energy close to love. If you try to feel grateful and negative at the same time, you will see that it does not work.

Be grateful for all that you are, for the abundance that you are. Stop taking things for granted. We are so accustomed to the good things in our life that we don't appreciate them fully. That surely includes ourselves. We do not appreciate, respect and love our own selves enough since we take for granted the unique sacred miracle that we are.

*"The more you recognize and express gratitude for the things you
have, the more things you will have to express gratitude for."*

—Zig Ziglar

Every morning as you open your eyes, be grateful for the good night's sleep, or at least a part of it. Be thankful for being alive and well to start the day. Appreciate your body and each part of it, for your lungs, your digestive system, and your muscles and tissues that allow you to move. You will automatically receive more things in life for which to be grateful. You will know true abundance.

As my favorite talk show host Oprah Winfrey says: "*When you are present in gratitude, you awaken the bigness of even the smallest things in life. You make yourself the richest person on earth.*"

Author Melodie Beattie writes:

> "*Gratitude unlocks the fullness of life,*
>
> *it turns what we have into enough and more,*
>
> *it turns denial into acceptance,*
>
> *chaos to order, confusion to clarity.*
>
> *It can turn a meal into a feast,*
>
> *A house into a home, a stranger into a friend.*"

I cannot describe it any better. When you feel gratitude, nothing around you changes, but "you" change. It shifts you and that is what we aim for in this process.

To me, author Louise Hay is the master of Gratitude. The way she radiates and expresses thanks for all that is, is so inspiring. Any book or work of hers is based on abundant gratitude and self-love. She was my very first inspiration for this work and I still recommend any of her books to my clients, daily.

Exercise 7:
Mirror work

Why not do the exercise of the mirror once again, now with an attitude of gratitude? The only opinion that counts is the opinion you have about yourself. Now we can take this further, leave the opinion behind and be grateful.

Look in the mirror and smile at yourself. Be grateful for what you see, as every single line in your face is a testimonial of your journey. Be grateful to be you. You are special; you are worthy. You have the right to be yourself and to love yourself.

Look at yourself and see yourself as a survivor, as an expression of your soul, as a source of beauty, designed perfectly and maturing naturally. Look into your eyes and see the seat of your soul. Feel the appreciation, the acceptance, feel the gratitude.

Exercise 8:
Gratitude journal

Keeping a gratitude journal is the best exercise you can do for yourself, day in and day out, to help you shift out of chronic stress. When I started my journal, I never thought that it would be that powerful. To write down every day at least five things or people or situations that you appreciate will change your life. It surely has changed mine. You might struggle with this in the beginning because we live a negatively programmed life, always looking at scarcity with a judging or victimizing consciousness. It is a complete shift in awareness to go within and identify five positive statements every evening. By choosing the feeling of gratitude and the daily repetition, you will slowly break the pattern of scarcity (poverty mentality) in your subconscious mind. Take a journal and make it your special booklet, with pictures or anything in it that makes you joyful. Practice gratitude every day for the next three months and you will never want to stop.

How does one love oneself practically?

My clients ask me often "how" they can love themselves. They want to know how one can do that in a practical sense. Is it not amazing that we know so well how to love other people, but we have no clue when it comes to loving our beautiful self? The question is to be answered in line with Buddha's wisdom: "How do you love anybody else in this world? In the energy of love, you can do to yourself what you do to others." Just "love" yourself, either by sending yourself loving energy, by giving yourself extra attention, by making quality time for yourself, by taking good care of yourself (see Chapter 10 on Self-Care), by giving yourself a compliment or a present. In whatever way you send and show your love to your loved ones, do the same for yourself.

Exercise 9:
Expressing your love

Write down all the ways in which you show your loved ones daily how much you love and adore them. For example: buying flowers, giving a compliment, writing a little note. . . Make a commitment to choose every day a similar expression of love for yourself. Welcome any small shift you feel.

Put together your values, vision and mission and go after what you really want

"Don't ask yourself what the world needs, ask yourself what makes you come alive. And then go and do that. Because what the world needs is people who have come alive."

—Howard Washington Thurman

Now that you are practicing self-love, you have become so much stronger and powerful and can stand in your light. You have become more aware now of your real values, of what is important to you. Loving yourself is honoring each of those values and living by them.

It also means to go for what you really want in life. It is about fulfilling your mission in this world because you are here on this planet for a particular purpose. Why are "you" here on this planet? Once you begin to love yourself from within, this purpose will become clear. Embracing your beautiful self is finding out what that mission is and living it from your core energy, which is love.

When your life is filled with passion and purpose, you will never experience the fear of not being good enough again. The Universe will always take care of you. You will always "be" enough and "have" enough. Abundance will be yours. I truly and honestly can testify to this and so can many others.

For years now, I have been following my purpose and passion. There are many tools, courses and teachers out there who can help you find out what that is for you. In my work, I bring people to their core and loving self-care, and I help them find their passion. But the real work of creating a vision, a plan, and goals and making the commitment to follow through is not my specialty. People like Tony Robbins, Mary Morrissey, Paul Martinelli and Christian Simpson are skilled at teaching people how to find their vision and develop their plans and goals to achieve it. I also recommend Julie Ann Turner from Conscious Shift to do this work with you, because she is my idea of the epitome of honoring our highest selves. It is a life changing experience to do this work once you are ready for it. Please see Resources at the end of this book for all contact information.

Live out of love

From this moment forward, let yourself manifest the love that you feel deep inside, in who you are as an individual. Take up your place in this world and live a soulful self-loving life. Stop worrying about what everyone else thinks, says and does. Simply live out of love. When you love yourself, when you are in touch with who you are, all fear will disappear. You will live "your" life as it is your birthright and not selfish at all.

You will simply radiate love. Love will surround you everywhere you go. People with a consciousness of scarcity and fear will not look for you anymore. They will not come near you as they will find other victims and judges with whom they feel good.

Success, prosperity and health will flow to you naturally as the abundance of the world is magnetized by your serene presence and inner peace.

Exercise 10:

Your summary

Write down your summary of this chapter, describing what it means to make self-love your source. What have you understood from this chapter? Which part has given you strength? Which exercise is valuable to you? By writing it down in your own words, you will integrate it better. I even advise you to explain it to the people you live with or your friends. The more you express your view on this or what you have learned from it, the more you will master it.

 ## Remember to celebrate!

What exactly can you celebrate today? And how are you going to do that? Enjoy this moment of acknowledgement and praise yourself.

Please go to my website **www.shiftingoutofchronicstress.com** and let me know how you are doing. I will celebrate with you every step along the way.

Notes

Notes

Step 7

CHAPTER 10

Practicing Ongoing, Conscious Self-Care

"I have come to believe that caring for myself is not self-indulgence. It is an act of survival."

—*Audre Lorde*

*M*y life's journey before my illness was certainly a life of sensitivity, empathy, and giving. But it was to my own detriment. The decisions to always be a good girl and to help those around me who were suffering, became a mission of saving and rescuing others while giving myself away in the process. I know now that you cannot rescue or save anyone, and it is my life's work to make others aware of the choice they have. The choice lies between giving too much, depleting and draining yourself along the way, or giving from a place of love, caring for yourself and others naturally, without sacrifice.

The 7-step process in this book has shown you up until now how to take conscious care of yourself by taking responsibility, being honest and choosing your focus. Along with that, I encouraged you to be aware of your words and to unlearn disempowering habits and adopt new ones. Intense self-care naturally includes strengthening your relationship with yourself by loving yourself unconditionally. The final seventh step in this chapter illustrates the practice of self-care in daily life, from taking care of your mind, needs and energy to taking basic care of your body.

This chapter is about the practical care I started to give myself every day of my life since my illness. It is a never-ending practice that I still apply today. I hope you will see how essential it is and decide to do the same.

Put your own oxygen mask on first

Women are known as born caretakers, always putting ourselves second. We often think that it is our job to live for others, care for others or take their burdens upon us. It is not.

It's time for us all, men and women alike, to take our lives into our own hands and give ourselves the permission and the right to take loving care of our own basic needs first. Think about it. When you are boarding an airplane, just before take-off you get an explanation of how to use emergency exits and lifesaving vests and masks. Can you recall what they say about the oxygen masks? The flight attendant strongly advises you to put the oxygen mask on yourself first, before you put it on your children or elderly relative. There is no better expression of caring than this one. This statement says it all. You can help others so much better when you help yourself first.

You will be a better mother, partner, friend, father, son, daughter, etc. if you take good care of your own needs first. Men are more naturally inclined to do this because they are the traditional "hunters" and know they must take care of themselves as head of the family. In my practice, where one of four clients is male, I find that men may have the same urgency to help and please others as women do, and will sacrifice themselves and their well-being along the way. However, in most cases, they do take better care of their own needs than women. Of course, that does not mean that they practice self-care "consciously."

So let's look at the warnings we receive when we are neglecting ourselves.

Listen to your intuition and listen to the signals

If there is one thing I have learned over the last 50 years until today, it is the fact that the Universe is talking to us all the time, but so often we do not listen because we think we know better.

When some people want strength and support from the Universe because they no longer have faith in themselves or think they need help from a higher source, they may pray for the guidance they need. Intuition also provides guidance. Intuition is when the Universe (or whatever name you prefer to give it) talks to us. The Universe is the voice that always knows what is best for us. It warns us when something or someone might harm us. It always does. But so often, we do not listen.

Every day of my life, my intuition is guiding me and yet sometimes it still happens that I do not listen because my head sometimes thinks it knows better. Every time this happens, I pay the price for not listening, either a little or big price. Have you been in a situation where your intuition told you not to do it, and you did it anyway? How did it turn out?

It was the same with all the warning signals my body gave me over the years. So often I had pains or felt exhausted. I thought I was taking good care of myself, eating healthy and exercising. But the self-care of listening to the signals of my body, mind, and soul, was not on my program. I ignored these signals over and over again, especially when I was overdoing it, going into overdrive. I thought I was superwoman and that I would somehow "manage."

Every symptom you get regarding your health is a signal, a warning you better not ignore. Your body, mind and soul are talking to you that way. It is often the only way to communicate with you since you also do not listen to your intuition.

From today onward, listen to your intuition, your sixth sense of what is nourishing you or depleting you. And keep a list of your symptoms as signals, asking yourself what your body, mind and soul are trying to tell you. You will be surprised by the answer you get!

Know your limits, set your boundaries

"Saying no can be the ultimate self-care."

—*Claudia Black*

Practicing self-care is knowing your boundaries, expressing them and respecting them. When I was bound to my bed for months, staring at the ceiling, I had a lot of time to think and reflect. If there was one thing that I was sure of, it was that I had not respected my limits. I kept on going no matter what, being blind to my limits, and never saying "no" to myself or anybody else.

When you exercise self-care, it is important to learn how to say "no," without justification. A "no" to yourself does not mean that you are weak or lazy; it means you are consciously choosing to hold back and balance yourself instead of putting yourself into a position that will deplete you.

Letting others know where your boundaries are is "your" responsibility. You cannot assume that they know your limits. They only ask for help, and you are the one who has a choice to say yes or no.

There is nothing wrong with saying "no" to people. "No" is a sentence. Honoring yourself and taking care of yourself is giving yourself permission to look within and see if it is OK for you to go ahead. Many of my clients find this to be one of the hardest things to learn, to set boundaries for themselves without feeling guilty. I advise them as follows: When people ask for something, you can tell them with a loving intention: "I will think about it, and get back to you later to give you my answer." Most of us have the constant habit of instantly saying yes, even if we feel within ourselves that it is not what we want. Asking for some time to think about it gives you the time to take your power back, to go within and check-in with yourself. You can answer with a yes or a no when you are ready.

If people take your no personally, that is their story, not yours. You have the right to say no and take care of your boundaries.

 Story:

It has been a hard lesson for me, too, to turn people down. In the beginning, people did not understand that I was daring to say no. They were used to having me always be there for them, always saying yes. Until I gave myself permission to tell my truth out of love and care for myself. Since I have practiced to love myself from within, every day of my life, I often say no to people without justifying my answer. People accept my no since they know I do it from a place of love. If they have a hard time accepting my no and judge me for it, it does not hurt my

feelings anymore when previously it made me feel guilty. No more shame or guilt or blame, as their reaction is their responsibility. I do not take it personally anymore.

Choose your own environment

Consciously taking care of yourself also means choosing with whom you wish to spend your time and energy. Stop being a people pleaser and trying to do good for everybody. It will drain you. Instead, choose with whom you want to spend your time.

Many people around us can poison our mind, body and spirit. You know who I am talking about. You can feel it. They drain you. They may seem to use you. Their energy is no match for your energy at all. Sometimes, we cannot choose with whom we spend time, like our boss or colleagues at work. It is imperative that you protect yourself from their negative vibrations and spend as little time as possible around them. You have already learned how to avoid taking things personally and how to say no. You will find multiple little shifts in this book that can help you deal with these people. Remember the snakebite story in Chapter 3, how you can turn the venom into your greatest lesson? Do the same with the toxicity of people, ask yourself what you can learn from this to move on.

Stay grounded when you are feeling surrounded by negativity. Keep yourself centered and remember to breathe. If necessary, do the grounding exercise in Chapter 5. Or visualize yourself enveloped by a big bubble of glass where nobody can get through.

After meeting or working with people who are depleting you, it can be very helpful to take a shower as soon as possible and relax a few minutes afterward, doing some abdominal breathing. You can re-energize yourself that way before you continue the rest of your day.

Whenever you can, surround yourself by positive people who are living their purpose and are living out of love, not fear. Stay away from drama and negativity. Stay away from everything and everyone that can potentially drain you. You do know if someone depletes you or if someone inspires you. You have the right to choose your companionship.

Balance your most precious fuel every day

Your energy is the fuel that drives your life. Take special care of it. No one ever explained the essence of this statement to me. Conscious self-care means to balance your energy input and output every single day, whether you suffer from symptoms of chronic stress or not. The energy you put out needs to be put back in. What you spend on energy and effort needs to be replaced if you want to stay healthy and live the life that you want. We underestimate the basic underlying logic and power of this principle.

Many clients who come to see me have low energy levels. They have depleted themselves for such a long time and are totally out of balance. When I ask them what percentage of their usual energy levels remains in their bodies, they often say around 20%. I am never surprised by this since nobody taught us this primary principle for a healthy life at school. When I first became ill, my energy level was less than zero, I am sure. I felt like a zombie most of the time, incapable of functioning normally. One wonders how we let our situation come that far. In fact, we often think our energy supply is endless, that it regenerates itself when we sleep. But we all know better. Sleep is important, yes, but so is rest and fun to fill the gaps in energy that results from our hectic multi-tasking lifestyle.

Our demanding society is obsessed with performance, prestige, and pressure. Combine these with speed and continuous availability and you have an ideal prescription for energy deficiency if you are not creating balance in your life. Nothing is more important than the balance in everything, but if you are dealing with chronic stress, I need to say that balancing your energy household is your priority.

For sure, the more you continue to dwell on the fear of not being good enough, the more energy will go into surviving by standing on your head for everyone. However, by taking loving care of yourself and feeling worthy as you are, you will regain much of that energy and feel extra energy coming freely from that place of love within you.

Choose conversations that matter

Energy is precious, and how we handle our energy is important. Just as we saw in Chapter 6 on how you use your words, it is imperative that you choose your conversations and what you are going to talk about. Talk to others about the things that matter, not to be right or to go into conflict. Go for a conversation that matters, that interests you, that gives you joy and that ignites your passion. Do not waste your energy or time on negative talk or discussions that try to prove you are right. That kind of discussion will deplete you. Practicing conscious self-care means to choose for yourself with whom you want to talk and what you want to talk about. Choose people with whom you can be authentic and empathic. You will not only regain a lot of energy this way and feel inspired, but you will also have a positive influence on others as they also feel your intention and energy field.

The 20-minutes golden rule

During my illness, when I began to feel a little bit better, I went to see a professor at the University Hospital of Antwerp who was well known for her knowledge in dealing with chronic stress-related illness. She expressed many uncertainties about my future, most of which I did not take in or accept. But there was one golden piece of advice she gave me for which I will always be grateful. She called it "the 20-minutes rule" and told me I would have to start using it at my own pace.

The 20-minutes rule requires that you do an activity, like setting the table, washing dishes, ironing, walking, conducting business, doing computer work, etc. for 20 minutes, using a timer to indicate when the time is up. After 20 minutes, you stop no matter how badly you want to finish your task. You take a rest for at least 20 minutes, lying on the sofa, sitting on the veranda, relaxing outside as you choose, but absolutely no activity. Then you start the sequence all over again, 20 minutes of activity and 20 minutes of rest.

Perhaps you can imagine how this illustrates the basic principle of balancing your energy level. Trust me, it works! You slowly build up some reserves again, never going over your limit, even though it is so tempting not to respect the 20 minutes. The stricter you are with this rule, the quicker you will see results, but it does take weeks or months of practice, depending on how low your energy level is at the start.

My experience with this rule has been phenomenal, although it was not easy to accomplish. I started off with 5 minutes of activity as that was truly all I could do at the time. Maybe I could have done 10 minutes, but I was not going to try. I set my limit at 5 minutes for at least the first month, before adding 1 minute more. Therefore, it took me a huge amount of discipline to respect my limits and commitments regarding this rule. Nevertheless, it did work well. I was able to build up my reservoir of energy slowly, day by day. I can say that I still use this rule today if I feel I am going through a very demanding time. It helps me to remember and respect my balance of energy input and output.

The following subsections are all related to finding balance within your body, mind and life.

Breathe

"Sometimes the most important thing in a whole day is the rest we take between two deep breaths."

—*Etty Hillesum*

We know now that self-care is about honoring your natural energy balance, and nothing is more natural to your body than breathing. However, it is remarkable how our natural breathing can be deconditioned. As a little child, we breathe from our bellies, which fill up with air as our lungs take it in. Growing up, we get more anxious and increasingly breathe from the top of our lungs, more superficially. We are often in a hurry or overdrive, never taking the time to get back to our natural state of rest, which I described in Chapter 2, "A Different Way to Look at Chronic Stress."

Breathing helps you to dissolve stress. Whether you are feeling tired, nervous or just taking a moment to relax after a long day, go within to feel what it is you need for yourself. Often intentional breathing is the activity that will give you a sense of inner peace. The increase in oxygen intake helps to relax the muscles all over the body.

We breathe unconsciously without realizing its power, and we do it about 20,000 times a day. Still, the nicest thing you can do for your body and mind is to breathe consciously. When you choose to breathe with an intention, you immediately feel a shift from your head to your body. The breath takes your awareness into your body. Your internal processes begin to slow down. Your heart rate, your racing mind, "everything" starts to follow the rhythm of your breathing, as if it gives a certain direction in life.

Breathing consciously does not cost you a cent. You can explore it and expand it along the way, naturally, without force or limitation. It will shift you from chronic stress to inner balance. See it as a "treatment" with which you can heal your body and your mind and experience freedom and inner peace.

Exercise 1: Just breathe

One exercise I give my clients uses the following sequence:

Lie down on your back (or sit down) and feel the different types of breathing you can perform.

- *Place both hands on the top of your chest, left and right, just under your collarbones. You can breathe from the top of your lungs, which is what most of us do all day long. It is very superficial breathing, however, and is the kind of breathing that will initiate hyperventilation when we are anxious or panicking. It can make us feel dizzy and weak. Just be aware of that type of breathing.*

- *Then place one hand on the center of your chest and one hand on your belly, and breathe deeply. You can feel which parts of your body are filled with air as you are breathing in deeply. Feel what your most natural breathing is. Most people only breathe into their chests, not into their abdomen.*

- *With the next step, you can now concentrate on the hand that is on your belly. You can start to learn to breathe with your abdomen, blowing it up like a balloon while taking in air. Breathing into your belly is the most relaxing breathing you can do. By inhaling through your nose and exhaling through your mouth, you can develop your own rhythm, whatever suits you most or feels most relaxing. You can do four counts breathing in and four counts breathing out. If that goes smoothly, you might want to breathe out for a count of 6 or 8, until your abdomen region is empty. Do not force anything. Just slowly make your hand move up and down. You will feel an immediate peacefulness within you.*

- *I suggest that you take up this last breathing exercise daily if you suffer from nervousness, bad sleeping patterns or other uncomfortable symptoms.*

Breathing is a therapy on its own for stress-related symptoms, although I provide only the basics here in this chapter. If you want to take your breathing further and deeper, you can go to a breath therapist or take a yoga class that includes "pranayama," the yogic breathing practice that has the same effects that I describe above.

Intentional rest and relaxation

My breathing exercises were the best way for me to get into a relaxed state when I was in continuous overdrive at the beginning of my journey out of chronic stress. I combined these exercises with relaxation techniques that are easy to use.

Relaxation means getting out of your head and directing your full attention into your body. You allow yourself to feel the body and all of its parts and let all of the tension go. You can do this in different ways, but the most effective one for me is to do a body scan.

Exercise 2:
Body scan:

Doing a body scan means literally to scan your body from top to toe. Lie down on your back (or sit down). Bring your attention onto each body part as described. You can start from the top of your head down to your forehead, eyes, nose, and mouth, including all of your facial muscles. You can move your attention down toward your collarbones and chest bone, feeling your chest completely relaxed. You can even feel your lungs and your diaphragm and go into your abdomen, where you can relax while continuing to breathe. Slowly release all the tension around your pelvic area and from there to your genitals. Feel the

> *muscles in the front of your upper legs relax and then let go of the tension*
> *in your knees. You can go down all the way to your feet and toes.*
>
> *Take a deep breath in and start now from the sole upwards via the back*
> *of the legs. Relax your calves and back of the knee completely and go all the*
> *way up to your big gluteus maximus muscle in the buttocks, which makes*
> *you feel heavy and completely embodied. Now you can allow yourself to*
> *feel your whole back with its spinal column, ribs, and shoulder blades.*
> *Let go of all the tension in your neck area and feel the back of your head.*
>
> *Stay completely relaxed a few minutes until you are ready to move your*
> *hands and feet, then slowly come up to continue your day.*

You can also have a simple rest, lying on a sofa or the grass outside and distract yourself from your busy mind. Maybe listening to some music or visualizing your next holiday. Let this peaceful moment take you away from the busy conversation in your mind or your tired body.

Give yourself the rest you need, even if it is in the middle of the day. In my family, we have always integrated siestas on the weekend since we lived in Africa, where everybody takes a break around lunchtime to escape the heat. In Spain, they do the same. So once we were back in Belgium, we continued to apply this pleasant rule, and it can be very useful. Just having a rest with the intention of letting go of all your worries and deadlines has a balancing effect on your mind and body.

Sleep

One of the first signs of dealing with serious stress is a disturbed sleeping pattern. Whether we cannot fall asleep easily or we battle with real insomnia, we often toss and turn while our busy minds prevent us from having quality night-time sleep. Of course, our energy level during the day, and also our full daytime alertness, may suffer severely from this.

In my life, restoring a deep sleep has been one of the hardest things for me to do because my whole system was completely dysfunctional for a long period. For months into my illness, I could not find any sleep whatsoever and, therefore, I was totally exhausted, mentally and physically. To me, there is no worse torture than being unable to sleep. It is a vital automatism that you cannot control and, unfortunately, you only realize its value when you have lost it.

Not sleeping is not advisable and although I am against most medical "pills" as a treatment for any health issue, I advise all of my clients to consult a healthcare professional when it comes down to serious ongoing sleeping problems.

Conscious self-care includes a regular sleeping hygiene that you put into place and follow strictly. This includes:

☐ *Establishing a regular relaxing evening and morning routine.* Try to avoid emotionally upsetting conversations and activities before trying to go to sleep. Don't dwell on problems or bring your problems to bed. It is advisable to go to sleep before midnight, between 10 and 11 p.m. Try to wake up at the same time every day, weekends included.

☐ *Avoiding stimulants such as caffeine, nicotine, and alcohol too close to bedtime.* While alcohol is well known to accelerate the onset of sleep, it disrupts sleep in the second half of the night as the body begins to metabolize the alcohol, causing arousal.

☐ *Doing exercise can promote good sleep.* Vigorous exercise is preferably done in the morning or late afternoon. A relaxing exercise, like yoga or taking a walk, can be done before bed to help initiate a restful night's sleep.

- [ ] *Avoiding food right before sleep.* Stay away from large meals close to bedtime. It is sound health advice to have no food three hours before bedtime. Do not start experimenting with spicy dishes. And, remember, chocolate contains more caffeine than even coffee.
- [ ] *Ensuring adequate exposure to natural light.* Spend time outside during the day because light exposure helps maintain a healthy sleep-wake cycle.
- [ ] *Associating your bed with sleep.* It's not a good idea to use your bed to watch TV, listen to the radio, or read. Only use your bed to cuddle, make love and sleep.

If you combine these tips with all the other self-care practice that I advise in this book, you will surely restore your sleep. However, do not be surprised if it takes time and patience.

Movement

The balance of the body and mind also means engaging in some exercise. Life is movement. If you don't move, you don't live. It is amazing how we have become non-movers in the last 30 years. By living this sedentary lifestyle, we do not take into account that our body is designed to run, to hunt, to play, to jump. Most of us sit as much as we sleep in a single day. That is not in line with our natural design.

We do not move naturally anymore. Few of us walk to the shops, take the stairs or go for a walk at lunchtime. Yes, we force ourselves to move after a full day of sitting. We may go for a run on a treadmill or cycle on a stationary bike while watching TV. Exercise has become mainly artificial.

I advise my clients to exercise at least 3 to 4 times a week for an hour. In fact, we are very happy to have fitness centers with all kinds of fitness gear here in Belgium, especially during the time of year when it is dark and cold outside. And if this kind of exercise is part of your life, I sincerely respect you for it. It takes a lot of discipline and perseverance.

However, it is your most "basic" movement that I want to encourage you to do. Do you walk outdoors in your village or town? Do you play outside with your kids or partner? Do you go for walks in nature?

All my life, I have been a sports fan. First horseback riding, then tennis, squash and golf, even running and fitness. Whether it is for leisure or competition, your motivation needs to be having fun and engaging in movement. I remember that, at a certain stage in my life, physical exercise became like a drug for me as I "forced" myself to be better, quicker, and thinner. I compared myself to others and slowly but surely started pushing myself too much, asking too much of my precious body.

It seemed quite normal at that time, but what I see now is that people either do too many sports or too little. Rarely does one find a natural balance. When I was recuperating slowly from my illness and immune system breakdown, I needed to move my body slowly but naturally. I committed to finding a natural sport that would balance my body, mind, and spirit. Then I discovered yoga.

Yoga has saved me from boredom and going nuts when I haven't been able to engage in sports as I did previously. I concentrated on stretching, muscle tone and relaxation first so that my flexibility increased. And I did not go into overload as before. Yoga is efficient in helping you to regain your energy and flexibility. It focuses on breathing with each posture and encouraging relaxation, too. Practicing yoga influences all of the physiological wonder systems in your body.

I did a bit of yoga every day while slowly building up my walking and stair climbing. Yoga is a practice that involves mind, body, and spirit, and I experienced it as the complete form of exercise. It took care of my whole "being" since so much spirituality is woven into it. I practice it almost daily, with love and compassion for my body and with the right intention to avoid forcing anything. I advise all my clients and friends to do yoga. But if you are dealing with any form of back problem, it is best to speak to a professional first or a yoga instructor with experience in alignment.

The more you spend time in nature, breathing and moving, or even just sitting quietly looking over the water, you reduce your inner stress. The stillness and the opportunity to feel one with nature opens the mind and the spirit.

The American author and trainer Anthony Robbins is a great supporter of movement and exercise. He says emotion is created by motion which means that the more you move, the more you feel. You need to breathe and move to feel more energetic and less tired. Start today, always respecting your body's limits, which can be different every day.

Food for your temple

Your body is your temple. You have only this one body for your whole life. Then why would we take such poor care of it and not nourish it well?

At the beginning of this book, I mainly discussed how you feed your mind. But, as I always say to people: You are not what you eat, you are what eats you! This statement refers to the fears and beliefs and all other poisons in our minds that may degrade us. In this part of the book, I want to talk about how you feed your body.

Many of my clients take better care of their cars than they do of their bodies. I have never understood that. And since my illness, I talk to my body every day and thank it for all it does for me automatically. And I feed it consciously with the foods and the beverages that it needs daily. This chapter would not be complete if we left out nutrition, which is an important source of energy as well as an essential part of self-love and self-care.

It is imperative to realize that the quality of our daily food intake plays a major role in avoiding and healing stress-related symptoms and diseases.

Take responsibility for yourself and be honest from within. These two first steps in this process of shifting out of chronic stress, should be applied again here regarding your food intake and energy balance.

Exercise 3:
Journaling:

Ask yourself the following questions:

- *What are my food habits? Am I eating the same foods every day, and making the same recipes over and over again every week since my upbringing or since I have lived with my partner?*
- *Which foods are beneficial to me and which are not? How can I find a balance in my food choices?*

Become "conscious" of what ingredients your meal consists of and how much of them you eat.

You are a unique human being, and I believe we each have unique needs for certain nutrients. A nutritionist can certainly help you to find out what your body, with its unique composition, needs to perform well and stay in balanced health. If you feel tired, for example, you may require certain nutrients to get more energy. If you follow your inner voice on what is healthy for you and what is not, it will likely be quite accurate. Your body, stomach or digestive system might tell you which foods help your body to stay healthy, which foods are not as welcome as others and which may drain you.

One thing I know for sure about my body is that sugar is not good for me. When I was ill, I did some major detoxes and diets for different organs, but the biggest detox I did (the best decision that I made) was to completely cut out the use of sugar.

For seven years, I did not have one ounce of sugar or products containing sugar. No desserts, sweets, bread, cakes, biscuits, alcohol—nothing that contained sugar. I know deep within that my body reacted well to this change. Slowly but surely, my results were obvious. Meanwhile, I have again allowed sugar in my diet for the last nine years. I can enjoy a glass of champagne or wine and eat a dessert on occasion, but when I do, it is just a treat and not a habit. I do not need it nor do I overdo it in any way. Finding the balance is the key.

Fruits and vegetables are my favorite foods. In my practice, I often see people asking so much of their bodies and minds but they live on pre-packaged processed foods, bread and meat day in and day out. What can be more nourishing than fruits and vegetables brought forth from our Mother Earth? Are you eating fresh foods every day? Are you taking in all the vitamins that veggies contain? Do you eat green veggies every day?

As I said before, there is so much information out there about which foods contain which ingredients for treating which deficiency. In general, we need to choose a variety of foods every day, and preferably fresh ones. Eat foods of all colors, surely including the red fruits and green veggies, which contain essential nutrients. Listen to your body's needs.

☐ *Which foods satisfy you more than others or which ones make you feel bloated?*

☐ *Are you OK with raw foods or do you prefer them steamed?*

Personalize your daily intake. Remember to be aware of your food choices and just do the best you can without judging yourself for it.

A note on natural food supplements:

Please be aware of the deficiency of vitamins and minerals in our daily food intake. Ever since I had my serious stress-related illness, I have been supplementing specific elements to my normal meals daily. Again, this extra supply can be different for everyone, and also depends on where you live, and what lifestyle and body composition you have. In the early stage of my recovery, I even needed magnesium through infusion as I had a serious deficiency that could not be resolved by oral supplementation. It is advisable to consult a specialist to help determine which supplements you need to balance your input and output.

Water

One of the simplest methods of profound self-care is to drink enough water every day. We all know that our very first need to stay alive is oxygen, but surely you can put water as number 2 on the list. It regulates your body temperature, 24 hours a day, seven days a week. Water helps you to absorb and digest food, and it helps your body to eliminate all the toxins from the environment. Most processes within our bodies depend on it. In fact, about two-thirds (60%) of the human body is composed of water and our blood consists of about 90% water.

Start to see water as a necessity for your wellbeing. You need at least 1.5 l of water, depending on your body composition, environment, and lifestyle, each day. Try to consume a pitcher full of water each day. It is not advisable to drink a glass of water before you eat a meal because it dilutes your digestive juices. However, it does reduce feelings of hunger because the brain does not know the difference between hunger and thirst. You will overeat less if you drink enough water daily.

> Important note: This book has no intention of telling you what you "should" do or not do regarding your daily intake, or regarding anything else, for that matter. I sincerely believe it is important and imperative that you, yourself, take responsibility for getting to know your body well enough to embrace and fulfill its needs. In that way, your body will function at its best.

Living in the now, stop "doing," start "being"

"*Just be, right now, here; and breathe. Begin to trust the magic of yourself.*"

—*Nikki Rowe*

Living in the present is a challenge we all face. There is always a distraction. Life right now is never enough for most people. So many clients of mine are always after "getting" something, getting a perfect life, even though that means consistent postponing and not living in the here and the now.

As we have seen in the course of this book, so much of our cultural conditioning pulls us out of the present moment. We hope to have in the future what we currently lack, meaning that we assume the present to be insufficient. It is through awareness and being in the present moment, being grateful for it, that we find our completeness and balance.

We are too busy doing, not "being." Living in the now with our challenges and obstacles gives us the essence of being centered, secure, peaceful, unconcerned and yet aware. Being in the present moment will give you the appreciation and the joy of simply being here.

You can best learn this through meditation, you can meditate while walking on the beach or in the forest. But daily practice of sitting meditation in silence is a basic advice that I give to my clients to increase their balance and well-being.

Meditation

"The thing about meditation is: You become more and more you."

—David Lynch

Silence is the only way to get in touch with yourself. In the chapter on habits, we have seen how important it is to listen and be quiet and empathic instead of talking. In this chapter, we bring that practice of listening to an even deeper level, to shut down the most noise in your head.

This self-care practice is done in a quiet space where you will not be disturbed. You can create your private, sacred space in which to do this. Maybe you want a candle and some extra cushions nearby. Or you just want to have a comfortable chair to sit up straight with your feet on the ground so you can feel connected with the earth through both feet.

Sit comfortably and close your eyes and become silent within. You can concentrate on your breathing again or say a mantra while you sit quietly. Let go of all attachments to your thoughts or words in your head. Deepak Chopra calls it settling down the turbulence of the internal dialogue. You become a witness to your thoughts, of the noises inside and outside, nothing more, nothing less. Just witness and breathe.

The German writer Franz Kafka wrote:

> *"You do not need to leave your room,*
> *Remain sitting at your table and listen.*
> *Do not even listen,*
> *Simply be quiet, still and solitary.*
> *And the world will freely offer itself to you to be unmasked,*
> *It has no choice*
> *It will roll in ecstasy at your feet."*

Many spiritual leaders encourage us to meditate every day. The spiritual teacher Marianne Williamson says that the only way to move out of fear is through spiritual practice, namely a consistent practice of forgiveness, a consistent practice of meditation and a consistent practice of prayer. She continues to say that this demands consistent devotion and dedication and most of all a lot of emotional and mental discipline.

I could not agree more. It is clear that we cannot dissolve all our fear and stress if we do not decide to travel inward to make the outward journey. This is what this book is all about. If you were experiencing chronic stress when you started reading, you now have a lot of tools to make the journey inward and build a strong foundation for a long-lasting shift away from chronic stress.

Daily meditation takes discipline and perseverance, but it is so worth doing. Since it has played a major role in my recovery and my consciousness, I have become a meditation coach through the Deepak Chopra Centre and practice it every day. It keeps me in touch with all that I am and with the miracle of life.

Recently, Deepak Chopra has partnered with Oprah Winfrey to give meditation challenges online, called "Oprah & Deepak 21 day Meditation Experience." They do it a few times a year, and I found it one of the most precious gifts you can give to yourself. It is a free gift; the only thing you need to do is enroll and have the discipline to do it. It is worth your while to try it out. It is a life changer.

You can see this particular self-care as taking care of the soul. It is a way of life. See yourself as the Universe, as one with everything that lives. By taking care of "you," you will take care of everything else.

Me-time and fun

Including "me-time"–time for yourself–in your self-care practice every day is non-negotiable. It is so obvious, yet why do we have such a hard time to make it a priority? Again, it is the conditioning of seeing me-time as a selfish concept that makes us postpone it as long as we can until it is necessary. Only then does me-time seem justified in relation to others and ourselves. While taking me-time is again your birthright and not at all selfish, you can completely recapitulate all that we have said about self-love and justify me-time within that frame. Similar to loving yourself unconditionally, taking that special me-time to get back into balance will certainly make you a better parent, friend, worker and citizen. It is so healing for your soul to take time for yourself, to take the time you need to rebalance your energy level and emotional level.

During that me-time, you can do what you want or just "be" and do nothing. You can go back to activities that make you laugh like a kid, bringing the child within you alive as we saw in the chapter on self-love. But "not-doing," or doing nothing, can be just as freeing. Try taking some distance from all your duties and just stand in your light, embracing the person you are and taking care of your needs. That is what me-time is all about: leaving all the judgements and guilt behind so that you can listen to your own feelings and needs and take a step toward fulfilling them. Do not forget to give yourself some self-empathy along the way.

Tapping—an SOS technique

As a therapist, I maintain an open mind for all techniques out there that may help my clients treat and heal any negative patterns, emotions or symptoms. I have studied many different techniques and Emotional Freedom Technique (EFT), in particular, is one that stands out for me and that I have practiced and also taught to my clients. It is also known as "Tapping."

This easy-to-use method was founded by Gary Craig, the creator of EFT. You can do it by yourself or with a coach. Gary Craig says that the cause of all negative emotions is a disturbance in the body's energy system. As we saw in Chapter 2, our bodies go into continuous fight-or-flight response due to repetitive little internal and external triggers that affect our emotions, usually negatively. The EFT method halts that response and reprograms the brain and body.

The EFT sequence hits all the major meridian endpoints that you can tap with your fingers. Many studies have shown its effectiveness in treating major disorders and issues. I found EFT especially useful in emergency situations such as anxiety, panic or fear. I have even used it with severe pain, and it does work to relieve it. Nick Ortner, who has been an EFT expert for years has launched this concept worldwide as "Tapping." If you are interested in learning more about how to use EFT, you can find the appropriate link in the Resources section at the back of this book.

Let "Conscious Self-Care" be your daily practice

Surely there are other ways to take care of your body, like a good full-body massage, a Reiki treatment or many other modalities that can help remove toxins from your system. My intention for this last chapter and in this book has been to talk mostly about "natural" self-care that "you" can practice daily. Meaning, the care of yourself that you can choose on a daily basis, without the need for anyone else. For example, making time for yourself to take a good, relaxing bath with candles on the side, or to sit on the grass barefoot and observe everything around you with gratitude.

Or just plain treating yourself as you would treat your best friend. That is what I mean by taking care of yourself.

Daily conscious self-care is your responsibility, and you already have everything you need to take excellent care of yourself. I see this as your duty and privilege at the same time to honor yourself that way. Enjoy your self-care every day, honor your temple, honor who you are.

Exercise 4:
Your favorite:

What particular self-care aspect appeals to you most in your own situation? How do you want to integrate it into your life?

Exercise 5:
Your summary:

Write down your summary of this chapter, describing what it means to practice ongoing conscious self-care. What have you understood from this chapter? Which concept are you going to apply to your life or talk about to others? By writing it down in your words, you will integrate it better. I even advise you to explain it to the people you live with or your friends. The more you express your view on this or what you have learned from it, the more you will master it.

♡ *Remember to celebrate!*

What exactly can you celebrate today? And how are you going to do that? Enjoy this moment of acknowledgement and praise yourself.

Please go to my website **www.shiftingoutofchronicstress.com** and let me know how you are doing. I will celebrate with you every step along the way.

Notes

Notes

CHAPTER 11

The Best is Yet to Come

"A bird, sitting on a tree, is never afraid of the branch breaking because her trust is not on the branch but on its own wings."

—Unknown

I lovingly want to start this last chapter with this quote that my youngest daughter once gave me in challenging times, assuring me that I would manage whatever happened next. The quote surely illustrates the essence of this book and its subtitle.

Now that you have come to this last chapter, I want to congratulate you for having gone through the complete 7-step process. I have read somewhere that many people never finish a book they have so courageously started to read. I especially want to honor you for finishing!

I am convinced that the 7 steps have given you tools and insights with which to handle your chronic stress better than ever before. For those of you with a fear of not being good enough, this has certainly shifted for you. And your worries and anxiety about the daily circumstances in your life have probably taken on another dimension. Surely you can now live more in balance and from a place of inner strength. As the quote says, if you have regained your inner trust about who you are and how valuable you are, you can choose how to handle the unexpected, knowing that all the wisdom you need is within you. You can heal and live your life in your own unique way.

"A life lived by choice is a life of conscious action. A life lived by chance is a life of unconscious reaction."

—Neale Donald Walsch

How to take conscious action

Whatever you do, do not leave it at this. You have a choice because this is "your" life. Choose wisely how you want to spend your precious time. If you choose change, if you keep on practicing the 7 steps, you will see that the best is yet to come since it is practice that will make all the difference. I can testify that I still live by every single step every single day, and it keeps on building my foundation of authenticity and consciousness. For me, it has become a continuous and consistent habit to practice self-love and self-care, which automatically includes the first 5 steps of this transformative process. Whatever step you decide to focus on, you can be sure it will always have a serious—and beneficial—effect on your overall well-being.

You can return to the book again and again. You can read through each chapter again as you wish, or just open it randomly and read that particular section because you are often guided to what you need to read. That habit works well for me with some of the best books I have read (and continue to read).

Maybe you can encourage someone in your life–at home, at work, among friends–to read the book, too. Maybe you have found someone with whom you can practice.

My questions to you now are:

☐ *Which exercise or story or chapter has helped you the most?*

☐ *Which step is still difficult for you to apply?*

☐ *Where do you need extra help to get a better result?*

If you want to let me know what the book has done for you, I will welcome your comments on my website.

Please go to **www.shiftingoutofchronicstress.com** and leave a comment that I will read personally.

Conscious action that takes you to the next level

➤ Assessment of your chronic stress level.

If you want to know the current level of your stress, I encourage you to go to my website **www.shiftingoutofchronicstress.com** and fill in the "Chronic Stress Assessment." I will get back to you in person within the following 48 hours with your results. These will give you a good idea of how your chronic stress level is affecting you today.

If you want to see the effect of practicing the 7 steps "after three or four months" and see how this process has changed your stress level and, of course, your life, I invite you to go to my website again and fill in the "Chronic Stress Assessment" once more. I will be happy to send you the results again and show you your progress.

➤ Free Discovery Session: "Shifting Out of Chronic Stress NOW."

If you are interested in starting to address your stress issues "right away" on a more detailed level with my help and personal attention, I invite you to go to my website and register for a free discovery session: "Shifting Out of Chronic Stress NOW." This free 30-minute consultation will immediately help you to get relief from your biggest stressful issue as I will personally attend to your needs. You will also discover what your next step might be in handling and shifting your stress. Please go to **www.shiftingoutofchronicstress.com** and click on "free discovery session." Then I will contact you within the following 48 hours to arrange a personal meeting.

➤ If you have a need to contact me in person for any particular reason during your journey out of chronic stress, please feel free to send me a personal e-mail message at **danielle@shiftingoutofchronicstress.com**.

Last but not least I want to "thank you."

I am grateful for having been a part of your life through this book, which is an important part of my life's work. May you love and care for yourself as well as you deserve and may your life be as balanced and fulfilling as you choose it to be.

"*You are your best investment.*"

Danielle

Notes

Notes

Resources / Alphabetical

Anthony Robbins, *Re-Awaken The Giant Within, (Robbins Research International, 2013)*

Charles Duhigg, *The Power of Habit* (Random House, 2014)

Dale Carnegie, *How to win friends and influence people* (Simon and Schuster, 1981)

Don Miguel Ruiz, *The Four Agreements* (Hay House, 1997)

Don Miguel Ruiz, *The Fifth Agreement* (Hay House, 2010)

Dr. Wayne W. Dyer, What do you really want for your children (20th Century Fox, 1985)

Dr. Wayne W. Dyer, *The Shift* (De verschuiving, Kosmes Uitgevers, 2010)

Eckhart Tolle, *A New Earth* (Penguin USA, 2010)

James Allen, *As A Man Thinketh* (Tarcher, 2006)

John Kehoe, *Mind Power* (Media House Publications, 1992)

Julie Ann Turner, *Genesis of Genius* (Creator's guide Press, 2013)

Les Brown and Paul Martinelli, *Empowering Mentoring Program,* 2011

Louise L. Hay, *You Can Heal Your Life* (Hay House, 1987)

Louise L. Hay, *The Power is Within You* (Hay House, 1991)

Marianne Williamson, *A Return to Love* (Harper Collins, 1996)

Napoleon Hill, *Think and Grow Rich* (Denk groot & word rijk, Verba Uitgeverij, 1994)

Oprah Winfrey, *Soul Sunday* (Harpo Productions)

Stress, Fight-or-flight response, *Free Wikipedia Encyclopedia*

Audio and DVD:

Anthony Robbins, *Personal Power 2* (Audio Program)

Paul Martinelli, *Power Principles (Audio CD Program)*

D. Chopra, S. Covey, T. Moore, Dr. B. Siegel, D. Whyte, M. Williamson, *Quest: Discovering Your Human Potential*, (Audio, 1996)

S. Covey, M.V. Hansen, T. Moore, G. Roth, Dr. B. Siegel, D. Whyte, M. Williamson, *Quest: The Spiritual Path to Success*, (Audio, 1996)

Ona and Les Brown, *Affirmacise Take II*, (Audio CD 2008)

Les Brown, *It's possible*, (Audio, 2011)

HSP, Highly Sensitive Person:

Elaine N. Aron Ph.D., *The Highly Sensitive Person* (Random House, 1999)

Elaine N; Aron Ph.D., *The Highly Sensitive Person's Workbook* (Random House, 1999)

Nonviolent Communication:

Marshall B. Rosenberg Ph.D., *We Can Work it Out* (Puddle Dancer, 2005)

Marshall B. Rosenberg Ph.D., *Living Nonviolent Communication* (2005)

Law of Attraction:

Rhonda Byrne, *The Secret* (TS Production, 2006)

What the Bleep Do We Know, DVD (ABC Distribution, 2005)

Bob Proctor, *You Were Born Rich* (Life Success Productions, 2002)

Esther and Jerry Hicks, The Teachings of Abraham, *Getting into the Vortex*
  (Hay House, 2010)

The Mind-Body Connection:

The Cure is. . .? Film DVD (Beyond Words Publishing)

The Connection, Film DVD, www.theconnection.tv

The Power of the Heart, Film DVD, Baptist De Pape, 2014

Values, Vision, and Mission:

Julie Ann Turner, *Genesis of Genius*, Power Arc, 2013
  (www.ConsciousSHIFT.Me), And Host of the Global
  ConsciousSHIFT Show (www.ConsciousSHIFTShow.com)

Emotional Freedom Technique (EFT):

Nick Ortner, *The Tapping Solution* (Hay House 2013)

Internet:

The American Institute of Stress (AIS), www.stress.org

National Sleep Foundation, www.sleepfoundation.org

Wikipedia, the Free Encyclopedia, www.wikipedia.org

About the author

$\mathcal{D}$anielle Sax (1961), physiotherapist, has helped thousands of people
overcome their chronic stress symptoms using physical and manual therapy. Since 2003, after conquering a
stress-related illness, she specializes
in coaching, mentoring and teaching
sensitive people by helping them to
help themselves with their struggle

in this demanding society. She has learned from the greatest masters
in the personal development world, and she continues to challenge
herself daily. She is passionate about motivating and assisting people
in their journeys of awareness, self-love and personal growth.

As a life coach specializing in stress, she has an international practice, gives workshops and talks in different languages about the real
cause of chronic stress and the importance of the practice of conscious,
loving self-care. This book is based on her 30 years' experience with
stress and its effect on our lives.

Lightning Source UK Ltd.
Milton Keynes UK
UKOW07f1818020316

269476UK00011B/52/P